Angels Among Us

C. Stanton

Dedicated to Sandra...my best friend, my guardian angel, my mom

You were and Still are my Number #1 supporter and Fan. Thank you for always being here and pushing me towards my purpose

We love you mom.... Until we meet again.

Love always, your Baby Boy

Acknowledgments

First and foremost, I must acknowledge my Lord and Savior Jesus Christ. Without God, nothing is possible. Thru him all things are, he is all that was, ever is or ever will be. He is beyond amazing, and a redeemer of lost souls. I love you with all my heart and my soul God. You are my Rock, my defense and my Mercy. Glory is to you on the most high. Thank you for guiding me along this journey. That Angels are Among Us. Thank you, I love you and can't thank you enough. I love you, I love you, I love you.

I am very blessed to have the amazing family and friends who surround me every day. Each and every one gives me the drive I've always needed to continue pushing for my dreams and my purpose. To use my gifts to touch the lives of other's every day.

Sometimes all you have to do is reach for the sky, to come to the light. To believe whole heartedly, that no matter how impossible the dream you may have. Believe and fight for it every day. Embrace the grind and the journey as it will lead you on the path of your purpose.

"Success is not to be pursued; it is to be attracted by the person you have become."

— Jim Rohn

"All that I am, and all that I ever hope to be. I owe to my mother."

— Abraham Lincoln

To my mom, I could not have wished for a better mother. You have changed all our lives for the better. Although, your time on this Earth was short. I know you are always here, always loving, guiding us as you always have. I am so blessed to have you as a mother and the love you have shown to your family to bring this amazing story to others. To share it to so many and to touch their lives through these pages. Thank you for all the many blessing you have given to your family, the love you continue to show. The truth of these pages......that Angels are Among Us.

To my dad, you have always been right there in my corner. A man short of words but never of love. Often tough love, "a realist" so to speak but you always helped me strive for more. To keep pushing and climbing towards the dreams I want. And I hope I've pushed you towards the better. Our thinking on life and dreams, that anything is possible. You have always been there when I needed you and never asked for anything in return. I'm forever grateful for the two best parents on the planet. What we lacked in life, you both always found a way. To push your kids to be the best we could possibly be. To always dream and follow your dreams, never giving up. Looking back and I know we had this talk. "Mom, Dad; how did you both make it?" And they answer with you both was Love. Thank you both for never being short in that department.

To my Mamaw, I can't say enough about you. You and mom were the glue that held us all together. One of the strongest persons I've ever known. You were always there for us and helped shape the traditions and values that shaped the characters of us all. Guiding us with your wisdom and care of what life is truly about. Thank you, grandma, for raising me right, for our alone time watching Life time movies on the couch. The Kentucky Derby, all the family dinners. Always opening the door to me as a kid, to walk down the street five houses down when mom and dad ran out of "Bllllaaack Pooooopppp" in my strangely Texan southern draw as a kid. Not sure where that came from, but it does benefit me in the singing department I guess. But more importantly, raising me a Wildcats fan. Go Big Blue!!!

To my grandpaw, papaw Curtis who I look and act so much alike. You left to soon, like your daughter but the legacy you left behind has shaped generations of our family and what life is all about. You were short with words, but when you spoke, they were filled with heart and meaning. Never an ill word spoke of someone and the most caring, giving person I have ever known. I continue to work towards being more like you papaw. Thank you for showing me what true life, richness and love is all about.

To my older brother Shane and the greatest pitcher, I ever saw. Not only because of skill but of the entertainment value every time you took the mound. It's easy to forget those moments, but the day mom passed away going thru the downstairs basement and finding all your trophy's. Dated and signed baseballs of no--hitter after no--hitter with all the strikeouts. Remembering hilarious stories of the mind games you would play against your opponents. And now full circle, it's amazing watching you raise your boys Bryce, Tyler and Hunter with your wife Shannon. Taking your knowledge helping them in sports but more importantly in life. You all will never know how much you have done for me and I hope you truly know someday.

To my younger brother Adam and his high school sweetheart Jess. It's an amazing thing how love works.

How we are all led to the moments we are supposed to go, and how in some of the most challenging binds us together. Adam when you were sick back in high school and Jessica showed her love back then like she does now. Raising your two boys Andrew and Carter. Carter with the greatest laugh I have ever heard, may you and Jess always make sure he never loses that. And to Andrew, it's like staring into a mirror every day seeing him. He reminds me so much of you as a kid growing up. I know mom is looking down smiling when it comes to all you kids.

To Autumn and Amber, tears start to come as I even think of you two. All us brothers were so protective over you both. Writing here brings me back to when you both were so little. Always playing together, and I thought it was so cool growing up having sisters, let alone identical twins. Showing you both attentions always, and spending time having a tea party or watching Ariel from the Little Mermaid for the thousandth time. But to me, it didn't matter just spending that time and seeing you both happy meant the world to me.

Now full circle seeing you welcoming little nuggets of your own. Autumn with Ethan or Casey's Mini--me, with that beautiful smile and piercing blue eyes. It always warms my heart every time I see his little face.

Amber with Franklin aka "Frank the Tank." Still to this day, I am both shocked and impressed with how a 1yr old could completely devour a smash cake the size of 5 full--size cupcakes. Not just devour but completely finish it in one sitting, with no problem. Amazing!!! And already living up to his legend. 😊

To Shannon, Jessica, Casey and Adam McClain. Thank you all for finding these amazing people in my life. It's unbelievable if you truly think about it, how we are all brought together and have found one another. One moment, one little decision from life and all these beautiful pieces would fall apart. Thank you all for taking a leap of faith, trusting your heart and believing in love. I could not ask for a better group to continue to love my brothers and sisters.

To Hunter, Andrew and Ashlee. At the time of my greatest weakness, my lowest point. You three showing those amazing hearts and smiles to me every time to your Uncle. I hope through these pages and some day you truly know what you mean to me. Thanking you parents for a simple picture of you three in my wallet so many years ago. Something so simple, could led to saving my life. Changing my heart, outlook and looking deeper into myself on what life is truly about. Still when I thank about it, and how one decision would not have brought all the following beautiful moments in my life I know have. Thank you always.

To Brian Larson and The Larson Family. What can I say Brian but what a hell of a ride. Life has not always been pixy dust, unicorns and rainbows. But through it all, you have always been a great friend and supported me to push for my dreams as a singer. If it wasn't for you, your mom, dad and Mike taking me out to Special K's for karaoke so many years ago. Taking a shy 21yr old kid, who believed deep down that his voice could touch people.

To push me up on stage to share my true passion, talent and love to the world. And I guess I need to thank the good people of Milwaukee, Wisconsin at the Miller Brewing Company for providing the refreshments that evening. That a karaoke slip with my idol Tim McGraw's

"Don't Take the Girl" turned in unknowingly would lead to these amazing adventures. Keeping dreams alive, and to continue on as we did as young kids. Touring the world, town to town playing music. Me, you and my dad on the tour bus.

Thanks for always being there and always making me laugh. Well, sometimes again Mr. Miller Lite gets in the way of you Mr. Larson. But without a doubt way more laughter than anything else. My mom and grandma has always treated you as family and saw your true caring heart. Which is nothing short of the reflection from your family. Thank you all and for "Larson always being Larson." "Classic."

To the whole Raines Family, what can I say but you all are my 2nd family. Kenny, Big Ken, Crystal, Holly, Nancy, Aunt Marge, Uncle Donnie aka "Hog Head" D.J and Grandma Raines who always called me "Clinton." How it all starts at 5yrs old with "My friend Kenny, My friend Clint." You have always been there with open arms, even in times when I was struggling thru life on what really mattered and what I really wanted. Thank you for always being there, making me laugh and making life a little sweeter. It's truly a blessing to think of all the amazing people and pieces that surround you every day when you really think of it.

Big Ken, you always taught me how to build a dream with your mind. How to take your hands as a carpenter, work hard and create your dreams from thought first. To finish your dream before you start. But also, how to avoid a 16--penny nail and nail gun at all cost. Thanks, D.J. lol. 😊 As well as when you're spending the night, and Pops is on the couch. Never go into a laundry room to drown out the sounds of snoring to get some sleep. Especially, if you do.

Don't place your head at the door swinging in, as this is not the alarm clock you want in the early morning. Also, when out in the woods sliding down a hill of leaves. "Kenny, always let your dad go first." If not, he'll be sure to send you a vine wreath sailing by your head…. within inches of your life down after you blaming it on "Lopez."

But you all shaped and molded me into who I am today. I wanted to thank you all and tell you how I'm truly blessed to have you in my life as family.

To Tara Minter and the whole Minter family. You all have always been behind me in pushing me to be the best that I can be. As a singer but more importantly as a person and my relationship with God. Thank you for showing me that family life and loving one another is most important. Staying together and pushing one another for each of your dreams, no matter how wild and crazy some of us are. Our times out at the property for Halloween parties and showing laughter through it all. Thanks for always treating me as family.

To Sondra, Don, Frank, Milani and the rest of the String town family. Those of you who remember me back when I use to sing at the Front Porch and Bw3's in Florence. You all support me so much to strive and chase my dreams. Thanks for always being so kind and showing me love towards my talents. And now it's led to this, writing a book. Who would have ever thought it. But that's the thing with life and chasing your dreams. You keep moving forward and goals change. Once you reach some, they evolve and move towards even bigger ones. Thank you all for always having my back, showing me love and support. I'm not even sure I truly deserve. You all mean so much to me.

To Edison Elementary, Ms. Roger's class especially. Thank you for reaching out and for the first time asked to speak in front of a crowd outside of family functions and weddings. Thank you for being so kind and showing love towards my music. Which now has led to this, a book which is about what my day of speaking was. Chasing dreams and living the life you want. Don't let anything stop you. How you all touched me and wrote individual poems and how "Walk in my Footsteps" touched each one of you. It almost made me cry, how a song did so much. I will never forget you or this moment.

To Katie Poe, you are an absolute angel. You have no idea what you mean for me in the final weeks leading up to completing this book. But I know now it's a journey that will continue the rest of my life. You are one of my guardian angels that has helped me along the way and I hope someday soon we can finally meet. Thank you for giving me advice and to always walk in faith. To follow my heart and watch for signs; both good and evil to make the hard decisions of everyday life. You are to kind; and a beautiful soul. I cannot thank you enough for being one of my angels, one that walks among us every day. Thank you, Katie.

To all of my family and friends, those I haven't mentioned specifically. You know who you are and how I feel towards each one of you. You are my rock and make life sweeter. I feel as you are just an extension of my family and love you all. You make my life so rich with funny stories, happy memories, wonderful times we have shared and those still to come. I thank you from the bottom of my heart. You push me to follow my heart, chase my dreams and to make the world a better place.

Introduction

"The walls we build around us to keep sadness out also keeps out the joy."

—Jim Rohn

The whole reasoning behind this book is to show people love and then through even the darkest of times we can find some meaning and good behind it all. But you can come out of it; you can become a better person and those around you that may be affecting your life. They to can become better people from each encounter, each event as well. Thru it all how interconnected we truly are. That one encounter, one relationship can lead you to the pathway that you're supposed to go.

That every day we're surrounded by angels, people in our life. Things, events, moments that can lead to miraculous daily miracles. And if you truly take the time to notice little things. Peering thru the cracks, the little details. Then you can begin to see where your life is supposed to led you. If we take a step back, release and let go of control. Of every aspect of our life and follow our hearts. Then listen to your mind on what we feel is right. Life will take you towards your purpose and what your heart says, what you feel and push you towards your dreams.

I think deep down we all deserve our dreams, and we all have different ones. That's what makes us all unique and special. How truly blessed and lucky we are to be given this life that we live. And if we take a moment just to put more energy into lifting the world up. Rather than to bring it down, how much brighter the world would be. How connected life, people and things are connected so perfectly. Beyond what our minds can grasp. How great it can be, and how dreams can become a reality if you believe first in your heart. Get your mind out of the way of one's heart for once and just believe in what is truly possible. That if we take a step back, look and notice. We may find an Angel in ourselves, or a special person in our lives. That life is full of purpose in all of us. That love is what binds us all together, full circle and that they're truly are Angel Among Us.

Foreword

When Clint asked me to write the foreword for this, his first book, I jumped at the chance. You see, I have become his biggest fan. Let me explain.

We met and became colleagues within the music industry, but the relationship quickly changed. Our conversations would turn from business to topics like family, life, and spirituality. We also became friends.

He sent me the galleys of this book you're holding, and I began to read it. Before long, it hit me that his voice was reading the book to me. The conversational tone of his writing is unique and exceptional. It is as though he is speaking with me one on one over a coffee in a corner cafe.

His visits to me in Nashville have been incredibly joyful for me and his book bring smiles, laughter, unbridled joy, excitement and even a few tears. Clint really shares his innermost feelings on these pages.

I hope you will enjoy Angels Among Us as much as I did.

Chris Keaton

Table of Contents

Acknowledgments iii
Introduction xi
Foreword xiii
Ch. 1. Family is Forever... 1
Ch. 2. Feeling of Loss.. 9
Ch. 3. Positive Thinking Can Go A Long Way........ 17
Ch. 4. A Mother's Love 25
Ch. 5. A House Full of Children 33
Ch. 6. One of the Hardest Things 45
Ch. 7. Visions... 59
Ch. 8. Taking a Leap 67
Ch. 9. Heaven on Earth 91
Ch. 10. Finding a Dream... 101
Ch. 11. Or so I thought 117
Ch. 12. A Chance to Start Over 137
Ch. 13. A City of Blue 143
Ch. 14. Accident is the Mother of Invention 149
Ch. 15. Lessons to Live by.. 167
Ch. 16. Waves Crashing a Return 10yrs Later...... 173
Ch. 17. A Book Finished…or So I Thought 189
"Walk In my Footsteps"... 196
Author Bio: 198
Reader's guide:.. 200
Index:.. 202

Ch. 1. Family is Forever

"The most important thing in the world, is family and love."

—John Wooden

I've always been a writer. I've known in my heart, and in the life, you live. You're a writer, able to express your heart and words thru emotion with a pen to paper... But before I start this story and lead into the details. I want to first thank my friends, family and my best friend, my mom. I'm by no means perfect, but who is? But I've always had a huge heart, caring for those whom I just met, surrounded by the love that life gives us and the miraculous stories that bind us together. I have not always sought purpose in this crazy world, but I have had events, described in this book that have changed me, my thoughts on life, the afterlife, our existence.....everything.

It can't be explained, other than by what I've experienced and through helping others through my pain. This is what led to this writing, and I knew going through it, this is what I wanted to do. I've had those, and certain situations, thinking's of Christianity, tell me I'm wrong. This can't happen, only God can do this. And I don't dispute it, at any point. I think in many ways. Doctors, scientist, Buddhist, all people, animals and all beings. Living things, all creatures I want to say, with my heart, I have never brought anyone to judgement. Nor shall I ever, I seek nothing thru this, rather than to help in some small way by showing each of you, Love. And to tell the amazing story and events thru words laid out on paper for you.

Love is the end goal. It is the purpose in life and the basis of this story. Even, writing these words. I'm brought to tears thinking back on everything that has transpired and reliving these moments for a greater good. Love is the one thing that binds us all, it touches all things, and even thru death remains. You feel it; you seek it always. It is one of the rare things in life, that binds all things and time together.

I and my mom were, and still are best friends. I lost her 10 and a half years ago at the time of this writing. But thru it all, I gained a better understanding of life. What our purpose is, how to treat one another and to always grow. We're told as kids, dream big and you can achieve anything you want. But as we grow older. Loss, heartache, everything takes pieces of that away. I believe that's why I wanted to be an elementary school teacher. I've always been like a big kid at heart. I love meeting new people and hearing the amazing stories that led them to this point in time. You never know what one person to the next is going thru and I try to learn something new from each experience.

Although, I have no children of my own, other than my three beautiful fur babies back home. Charlie a black and tan datsun beagle with epilepsy. But the last 3 years he has had less stress in his life, more stability and a seizure maybe twice. But don't let that fool you, I've never seen a dog enjoy car rides more than him. Smiling ear to ear, jumping in your lap, taking the wheel turning his head back at you with his mischievous grin. Honestly, if people are reincarnated in the afterlife. He most definitely was a Nascar driver, gocart enthusiast or a chauffeur of sorts.

Angel Among Us

Moose my golden boxer lab or at least that is what the kennel told me and my dad's best friend. He's a 3lb. lap dog, trapped in an 80lb. body. Always curious about anything and everything. And when he steals my dad's recliner at night. He loves to sleep with his feet in the air chasing squirrels and rabbits as he dreams running full tilt. Here's a fun fact, as he's in deep sleep late at night, and his lips lay to one side flapping. I like to surprise him with peanut butter under his lips as he dreams. It's too funny; he keeps his eyes shut most of the time licking away till it's gone. Then spins, wakes up and looks at me like "Dad, what happened to my peanut butter deliciousness." I used to do this with our two Boston terriers my brothers and sisters grew up with as well.

Then there is Roo, my mini pin who's an oversized one at that being 25lbs. And the ruler of the pack. All rescues, I believe he got his name as he's a bluish gray color and looks like a miniature Kangaroo. When he's cuddled up late at night under your arm and gets too hot. He likes to let you know how he got his name as he kicks with his back feet pushing you away. Definitely, was a kangaroo in his past life.

And my dad's chihuahua mix, named Gizmo. And I believe he got his name from the Gremlins movie back in the day early 80's, as he makes sounds that sound just like Gizzy in the movie. Too funny. He loves me to death, and I always call for him by tapping on my chest. Then he crawls and gets approximately 2mm from my face to let me know he's there for cuddles. For which I mess with him, blowing in his ear, as he playfully rubs his nose with his two front paws. Too cute.

They are my kids and I spoil them every chance I get.... Every year, I make them their own thanksgiving and

C. Stanton

Christmas dinner plates. It's a great tradition. Individual turkey, ham, stuffing, and even homemade cranberry sauce. And don't get me started when I come home and mention White Castles lol...And yes, most pet enthusiasts will say, "You can't do that." But their excitement and look in their eyes. Not to mention the twisting and dancing they do. You look at those four lil sets of puppy dog eyes and try to tell them no, it can't be done. Keep in mind; they receive these burgers with no onions. As all dog owners and pet lovers know this is a no, no.

I wish I had little munchkins of my own, I truly do. But as in this book, sometimes life does not go the way as planned.... And again, that's ok. Sometimes, hardships and hurt seem to be too much and that we can't take it. I've lost friends, family sadly feeling this way. It breaks my heart, as I was almost one of them myself. But in that moment of pain, anguish. I reached out, looked at my dogs, a picture of my nephews in my wallet and thought how much they love me. My grandma, my dad and I said "No." I was in so much pain and heartache I let dark forces in. I bawled my eyes out, looked for a bible my mom gave me and couldn't find it. I started pulling things up on google. Looking for guidance, love and help from anywhere.

I'm by no means religious, but I try to learn each day and understand our purpose in this life. I'm eternally grateful for the choice I made. To my dogs, my nephews that I hope someday they realize how much they truly mean to me. In that moment I felt embarrassed, ashamed, saddened, heartbroken. I will get more in depth with this later.

My life was falling apart at every turn. But I'm here to tell you, "Love is all you need." I still to this day keep one of my favorite bible verse in my wallet. Matthew 7:7. "Ask and it shall be given to you; seek and you shall find; knock and it shall be open to you." So true and words so beautifully woven together. I sought love, anything in that moment to why I'm here. And looking at my nephews smiling pictures in my wallet, crying in my kitchen with my dogs sadly looking up to me. I found the love I needed, fell to my knees, prayed and found a reason to stay longer.

I'm thankful to my family and friends every day. My dogs, to my family, two coworkers at the time especially Mr. Bill White and Miss (Savannah) Marsha. I can never repay or do enough for the love each and every one of you showed me. I can never show you both enough gratitude in what you did for me, and from the bottom of my heart, I'm eternally grateful each day. It was not the proudest of moments, this chapter in my life, but I don't shy away from it either. I own it and wish to share. As I believe each moment happens for a reason.

Even in the toughest times, there are no coincidences, nor accidents. We may not at the time understand the hurt, pain or reasoning. But, if we take a step back, take a different perspective, grow and turn the negative pain, heartache into good. We can find our purpose, making our life and the world around us a brighter place.

I knew after coming thru this, the love I showed for someone. And no matter what I did, it was never going to be enough to save our marriage. Any one way, you could hurt someone you love or once loved it was done. I was living it, breathing it every day but thru it all I had to learn to let go. I didn't want to, I always pictured finding "The One" and for it to be perfect. Live the perfect life, in my dream home, have a couple of kids and grow old together, each day more and more in love. But this like others before me just wasn't meant to be. It wasn't in the cards for me, to have that fairy tale ending. But, I like to think the best is yet to come, like a great dessert. Looking back now I'm at a point where I hope she's truly happy. That I did love her and wish her well in her next chapter of life.

Most may find it foolish or crazy to forgive someone that has caused you so much pain. But I had to learn to let her go, to make her own decisions. I had to learn to love Clint again, before I could learn to understand her, myself and this life as we know it. I'm proud of the decision I made and what helped me in my time of need. The steps I learned, the steps I was taught, the steps I still strive to take today and the many angels that surround us every day. That if we look hard enough, they will find us and help guide you thru. They will always lead you in the direction where you need to go.

I was almost one, a number, a lost soul. I felt I could take this hurt no more. Even now it breaks my heart, a tight pain in my chest. But I made it, I came out the other side, and I'm by no means perfect. We all have different battles we face each an everyday, and they will still continue. But I want all of you, even those I may never get a chance to meet, to know that I feel their pain and that when you least expect it. Someone is always around, put in the right moments, at the right time to lead you on the path you're supposed to go.

Life's hard! We all know this, but your outlook on it can make all the difference. That's why I feel I have a huge connection with kids, with my niece and nephews. Even with my sisters. I still see them today, as my mom's little angels. They still can do no wrong, picturing them as they were when they were little. Three protective brothers, watching over them.

Life is hard enough for kids today; they are the future. But their amazing outlook and excitement on life, we all can learn something from them. How to stay happy and excited about each new day. But now, them having munchkins of their own. I know my mom, grandma, grandpaw, everyone we've ever lost. They are still around us, guiding us, molding us all, smiling down through the clouds with love.

Losing a mother is extremely difficult. I know I wasn't the first to do so, and I know I won't be the last. Especially, when you lose them and it's sudden. No warning, and like a light switch there gone. But are they really? Are they truthfully ever gone, in this moment or is it a belief to believe in the unseen?

C. Stanton

Ch. 2. Feeling of Loss

"Goodbyes hurt the most, when the story was not finished..."

—Anonymous

2007 I was working a part-time job at a local bar in Florence, Kentucky. My hometown, 10 minutes just south of Cincinnati. I had just recently returned after the hardships and struggles of trying to make it as a singer/songwriter in Nashville or NashVegas as the locals would say. Thru some unfortunate events, mostly of my own, something kept pushing me to come home.

I would talk to my mom almost daily, and keep in mind my parents just 10 months prior learned of this little adventure I would take them on. It kind of went down like this in the kitchen. Which I've always been a big dreamer, a risk taker and for everyone to always chase their dreams. If you are passionate about something, and have a love for it, chase it. Never stop because you only fail when you do. Fail a thousand times, that's alright, but it only takes one idea, one time to be a success. My mom was the best teacher of this philosophy.

"Mom, Dad I want to move to Nashville and become a singer, songwriter." They both were in utter shock, and dismay. The reason is I never sang in front of them once, nor have they heard an original song, let alone a piece of poetry. But, I always felt in my heart it's my greatest gift to the world. Putting emotions and feelings on paper, touching people in a way in which it moves them. Being able to capture other thoughts, emotions and relate with them on paper and pen. It's truly a blessing and a gift. To move someone to laughter or tears, recalling a moment in their life, shaping the words as if it was written just for them.

That's a special gift, one my mom has passed down to all her kids, one I wouldn't trade for the world, "So mom, I want to thank you."

True my dad "I'm a realist speech" and bombarding me with a thousand questions on why I can't do it was sure to follow before I could get my words out. My mom though, looked at me and smiled. "Clint if that's what you want to do, you go baby boy."

Of course, they wanted to hear and for the first time in 10 years, I sang in front of them, in the very moment where I once stopped. Funny how life works full circle and pushes you in the direction your heart wants to go. Now, the story behind this, which I wouldn't change for the world. When I was 11 or 12, I decided, and again I get little moments or ideas in my head for doing something. I act on them immediately. Surprising someone with a flower just because, their favorite meal, baking a cake, etc.

So, when I was 11 or 12, on Mother's Day, I decided I was going to make my mom breakfast in bed. Then using the vast technology of the 80's and early 90's recorded her an original song and sing it to her. So yes, a tape recorder and the soothing sounds of Bon Jovi turned down just enough to have background music, and my vocals would make it like it was my own.

So, I did, and she absolutely loved it, but being a shy kid back then, hormones and not into the person you've grown into and having some doubts. My two brothers made so much fun of me, correcting me of my visions of grandeur, that I really thought I was terrible. I thought, I literally embodied a feline cat in labor, squalling thriving in pain ready to die. Quite funny now, what we think when we let other opinions change our perspective of ourselves, and talents.

We as a family always grew up listening to music, singing Christmas songs baking cookies. Listening to the Judd's in my grandmother's kitchen most early mornings growing up. There are so many great traditions, and memories made with my family that are just special. I again would not change a thing. Sure, we weren't blessed with riches like Bill Gates, Warren Buffet or Scrooge McDuck (Duck Tales reference for all the young'uns reading this book) but what we did have was love. The most two loving parents a kid could ever hope for. Amazing Grandparents and the family friends that surround us today, that are family as well.

I know many times I would ask, mom, dad how did you guys do it. Five kids eating everything out of house and home. We were just a big family, tall and always growing out of clothes growing up. Christmas', birthdays how did we make it. And the answer is "you find a way, if you love something or someone enough. You will find a way."

And that cannot be a more true statement than to me now. You always find a way. No matter what. We all go thru hard times, take the good with the bad. Sunshine and rain. It's a circle, but your understanding and outlook on life is what drives the balance. Someone will always have it worse than your roughest day. Help one another thru this journey called life, every day you can. You never know who's watching, what a five-minute conversation may lead to or how it may even save you from a wreck down the road. Or brightening someone's day, taking five minutes to hear their story could change your whole life. Can lead you to love, riches, a lost friend. But filling your heart with love, it will tend to lead you with clues on where your life needs to go.

Ok, back on point. So, after my kitchen performance, my two brothers bashing it and me wanting to crawl under a rock and die. Something kept telling me in my heart. If you love something, stay the course, don't ever give up and your purpose will always push thru and reveal itself. So, from that moment forward, I did. Now, mind you I would sing and write in my room. Never to get slightly over a whisper. I've never asked them if they ever heard me, but I'm certain they did. They would always pry open the door, opening it just fast enough to try to catch me off guard and ask. "What are you doing" and my response was always "nothing," nervously "nothing at all."

Now, again I don't tell this to make my brothers feel bad or anything like that. I thank them, they made me who I am today as a singer and songwriter. They made me want to become better. Especially, in the writing department always crafting my skills alone in my room. Just my pen, thoughts and paper but to me it's also a tool for healing. To reflect on events, hardships...whatever moves you at that moment. To touch others, connecting through a poem or song, to me is the coolest thing. To move someone you may not know, to laughter, joy or even tears is an amazing thing and greatest joy.

Which leads me into English class every time we had to turn in poetry in school. The teachers always chose mine, which I knew being a shy kid back then. Nervously gripping a paper in class trying not to slip up or mispronounce a line before crinkling it into dust. If only I would have known now, how much women adored it, I most certainly would have shown this skill earlier in life. But I knew I had something, these teachers all felt with my words on paper, that they wanted me to share something unique and special with the class. So again, I believe everything happens for a reason. Even times of pain, there is a reason behind it. Something we learn, to use it like I am with this book to turn that negative, into a positive. To help one another to make life here on Earth a better place.

So, let's flash forward a bit. My parent's dad Jeff a Union Electrical Worker, and my Mom Sandra being whatever hat the family needed at any given time but mostly that of being a mother. The greatest job title you can have I think is of being a mom.

Finally, on board for my Nashville adventure, residing from a current position and the comforts of home I decided to chase a dream. Life's too short not to. Not to be happy, not to reach for the stars and not to be happy with those you love, to pursue things you are truly passionate about. I think we all deserve the dreams we seek, were all you unique in so many ways. So, dreams can always be fulfilled.

Full circle, a month or two before I'm scheduled to make the 4 1/2hr drive south to music city. A local restaurant has a singing competition for a chance to win a Silver Coors's light radio in the shape of a guitar. This is one of my priced possessions, you would not think so, but it truly is. Weeks leading up to leaving, I had all my family and close friends sign a little message for me to wish me well. My mom's message is so true, perfect and to the point. That's how she was, so fluent and flowing with her words; it is truly an art form.

"Baby boy, always remember to keep God in your soul and a song in your heart. And always be a dreamer." Love mom. Never lose sight of who you are and where you come from. Always chase your dreams and never stop dreaming.

She also gave me a book by Tim McGraw and songwriter Craig Wiseman to go with his latest album, "Live Like You're Dying." It entailed the journey of making the album, authentic and true to the fans. Changing the path of other artist and creating a unique album with his long time touring band.

Along with this, I received a much smaller blue book. It was about one song on the album, and the album's title track Live Like You're Dying. Inside the blue 6" x 6" book had beautiful words from both Tim and Craig about how the song creation came about. The fight to put it on the record, and the beautiful poetic words that flowed easily from the song, into this book. At the time, Tim's father Tug was diagnosed with a brain tumor.

A special song being from my all-time favorite artist but what it means to so many people. How we should live each moment, each day as if we were dying. What would you do, who would you talk to, what wrongs would you make right before you're gone.

It went on to be number 1 on the Billboard Country charts, a Grammy Award for Best Male Country Vocal Performance, as well as single of the year at the CMA. Tim said of the song, "Of course this song is special to me, but I think it is special to a lot of people. The song to me is not about death; it's an affirmation about life."

It's a song about life, living to its fullest even when faced with its hardest challenges. On each page, they reflect on the song with beautiful images sharing what life should be. Young kids of all backgrounds and races, adults young and old. Laughing, enjoying life, the outdoors small blessings that we often overlook and take for granted each day. How we should take each day, love one another, and in times of need pick each other up. But what's added to these pages, is forever, eternally priceless.

My mom, on each page, wrote me personal messages which I read when I get a chance and think of it laying in my grandmother's china cabinet by the dining room table. I took it with me to Nashville and read it almost every day.

You have to understand; my mom has the heart of gold. She never met a stranger and could see right thru you if you were full of something other than daily dinner. But things happen, they are not always good, and you have to learn to adapt and overcome. Do the best you can, with the gifts you're given and keep dreaming. No matter what, the mind is a powerful thing and can help you overcome some amazing things.

C. Stanton

Ch. 3. Positive Thinking Can Go A Long Way

"We must be happy of what we got, when we pursue the things that we want."

—Ben Franklin

Although........

"You can't just be motivated. If you have an idiot and you motivate him. Now, you have a motivated idiot."

—Jim Rohn

Positive thinking is also a helpful tool. I know a lot of times, its truly hard, negativity hits you from all sides. But, if you try to spin it, look a little deeper into the possibilities of what's occurring in your life right now, I promise you there is a bigger meaning for a better good. Our bodies, minds and our thoughts can shape our reality.

One of my favorite motivational speakers is Jim Rohn. He has since passed but his outlook on life, the choices we make was truly amazing. He has one of my favorite quotes of all time. When someone is putting you down, or saying you can't do this or that, you can't reach your dreams. Remember this quote. "Never let someone's opinion of you, shape your reality."

Now soak in those nine words. Never let someone put you or your dream down. Never let them shape the reality you deserve and want. As coach Jim Valvano said in his famous ESPN Espy speech, "Don't give up, don't ever give up." "If you can laugh, you can think, and you can cry, that's a full day." That's what I've always done in life, and what my mom always believed in. Don't ever give up on your heart, your dreams and never settle. It doesn't matter the path you take or the length of time it takes to achieve it. This is what it takes to reach your dreams. It may take a life time, but when you go thru the journey, the path it takes you to get there is amazing. What matters is what you believe in your heart and love your dream like a child.

Although, I have yet to have children of my own and doctors say that I may not be able to. I'm ok with that, as I never looked at having children as a guarantee. That you will find a wife, and be given this amazing, beautiful gift. I always looked at it as a blessing and a miraculous miracle. That if some way, I was given this gift to bless my life I would welcome it with open arms.

But some are not given this in life, and I may be one of them. But I know the world is blessed in other ways. Adoption and amazing foster children needing loving homes. Me being a former foster parent myself, although challenging at times. I do not regret in helping children in any way, who thru circumstances outside their own are placed in the states care.

I want each and every one of you to know, when you lay down at night and wake each morning. People all around the world are sending prayers and helping in ways you may not see. If you can't give money or food, blood donations, give someone your time. I hope in the near future to revisit the foster home outside Louisville for the annual thanksgiving dinner and Christmas party to show my thanks. To give anyway I can.

Kids are so priceless, in their thoughts, words, and outlook on life. They say the funniest things. Their outlook and awareness at times, is beyond belief often throwing us adults off guard and often taking notice. We should strive each day to help them when we can and show them attention. In doing so I have found, they help change our thoughts of reasoning about the outside world. They keep us young, in laughter, in mind. And we turn back the clock just a bit, years of negative thinking of what the world is….and should be for us all.

Bonus:

"As you think, so you become." "For as he thinketh in his heart, so is he."

—**Proverbs 23:7**

Letter to my students at Edison Elementary in Dayton:

Below is the speech I put together for Ms. Roger's and the 3rd Grade class but I was so touched by everyone that I decided just to speak from the heart. They reached out to me to come visit and speak to her class about life and chasing dreams. Also studying my song "Walk in My Footsteps." Sharing their own interpretations of the song and poems to me which I still carry. The front cover which ironically was covered in butterflies, which later on in this book you will understand why this is significant as well.

Here, I share these words below:

C. Stanton

To Ms. Roger's and her 3rd Grade Class:

The secret to living, is giving. The secret to life is love. Give your heart, every day to your dreams. Every moment, every day. Part of the fun of working towards your goals and dreams, is crossing them off. Don't look back on your life and not give 110%. Now give every waking moment to capture your dreams. Failures will come, and hardships. But they only become failures, once you give up. I'm asking you never to give up. Everyone faces trials and tribulations. Sometimes up against what must seem like impossible odds.

I've been there all my life but what's amazing about this life is the journey. The process to get to where you are supposed to go. Life will not reveal your dreams for you. You have to look in the mirror and call your heart and soul out. I'm going to live out my dreams, from this moment on and tell yourself. Believe in every one of your dreams and start living them today.

My mom has always been the big dreamer. She was my biggest supporter. And the stories I share today, I know without a doubt she's still here, still around. Love cannot be stopped, even thru death, love continues. Love conquers all.

She never met a stranger. She loved you, and from that day you were family. She loved every day with her heart for people to see and with love.

Don't search for defining moments, make them. Force them out every day, every moment. Everything I truly believe, good, bad or indifferent, happens for a reason. Keep an open mind on what you think life is and watch for the clues that lead you on the path to where you're supposed to go. We don't have the mind capacity to foresee what the future holds. Or what this moment, this encounter is or means. Embrace it.

Sometimes in life, you have to fight thru things you hate, to live the life you want to live. It's never easy, but it's worth it. Obstacles are what shape you. It's the pain, hardships that challenge your heart and your dreams. It's all a test. To weed out those who aren't willing to do the necessary things, that others won't do.

To fight, reach down deep in your soul. To do whatever it takes. Anything and everything or die trying to achieve the life you want to live. No one will hand you, your dreams. Take it!!! Right now, from this moment, change your life and take it!!!

You have to be talented in every aspect of your life. Learn the necessary skills to capture your dreams. The time we use, to sacrifice what we are, to become what we want. It's worth it. It's worth it to your family, your friends. Don't waste another day, don't take it for granted. It can never be given back and can be taken in an instance. One wrong mistake be protective of the decisions you make. "Stand guard at the door of your mind." Jim Rohn. Don't let evil forces in. Live now for your dreams. Tell yourself, your heart and soul.

Today, I am_____. A statement from the bible. I am , that I am. Just ask, and then believe you are just that, that you want and dream about. You're worth it, to chase your dreams.

Write down your goals, right now. Write down (5) each day, what you want and fight for everyday till you get it. I do this every morning before I start the day. What do I want to accomplish, then mid-day I write a new list after those that are scratched off and deleted? 5 goals each day to reach one day closer to your dreams. You owe it to the unes you love, those around you but especially, you owe it to yourself. You owe it, to you. Don't quit, till you achieve it. Lose sleep if you have to and gain passion to capture it, every day.

Jim Rohn "You can have more than you got, if you become more than you are." Happiness is not what you receive in life, but it is what you become. Make a list of goals, your goals every day that you want to achieve. Start with 5, then cross them off. Even small goals you want to get done. Then move to 10, then 20. Till you have a full day filled with chasing your dreams.

Don't know the skill to get there, learn it. I personally listen to audiobooks or training online. I find it more productive listening to what I need to learn to become better and chase my dreams, while still being able to be productive at work. Keep your mind focused and your emotions in a positive state towards your dreams. And the universe will be pulled in the directions of your dreams.

The key to a brighter future is you. What will you do today, to move one step closer to your dreams? Break the cycle of your mind. You're taught as a child, to be that of a child. To think of life as anything is possible, to imagine your dreams, create them and to be child-like. Chase your dreams, be who or whatever you want to be. What do you want to do at any given time. What changes that mentality, that thinking? Life, situations and circumstances. I'm asking you to protect your mind, your imagination. Guard your thoughts and feelings with your life.

Difficulties and obstacles will come your way, training you for the next step, the next level. Pain is temporary, if you don't quit. Stay strong in your mind. Chase and be hungry each and every day. Once you start, you gain momentum. And that momentum will gain more momentum and so forth. Taking you one day, one moment closer to your dreams.

Life is too short, make the most of it to help each other, everyday. Don't look back 10,20 30 years from now and regret not going after it. One day all of this will end.

I love each and every one of you. Don't look back on a life unfulfilled. Your talents. Bring them forward for the world to share. Use your one opportunity, your one moment to do your best with the talents you were given. Don't have your dreams staring back at you in the mirror. With life coming to a close. Not living out your purpose, your dreams, yelling at you.

"We came to You!!!! We came to You!!!" Les Brown. You need faith; nothing can be accomplished without faith. Faith in God, a higher power, your spirit, your heart, yourself. Whatever you believe in, it all starts within you. Believe you can do it. Don't stop and fight till you accomplish it. Believe me, but more importantly, believe in yourself.

All life is here for a purpose. The trees, the water, the mountains and the stars. It is all given to you. Make this world the way you want it. Picture it, visualize every dream in vivid detail and live it in your mind every day, and never waver.

But love others. The more you do, the more you make sure that someone else is ok. God, the Higher Power, the universe will make sure that your needs are met and taken care of, that you're ok. The day you realize your purpose on this earth is a lot bigger than you. That's the

C. Stanton

day your life grows and becomes richer. "Don't ever let someone's opinion of you, shape your reality." Jim Rohn/Les Brown

Ch. 4. A Mother's Love

"All that I am, and all that I ever hope to be. I owe to my mother."

—Abraham Lincoln

As with most of us life has curves and forks in the road. With my mom and my family, we are no different from anyone else. We all have struggles that may not be the same, but they are present. My family more than anything, our parents showed us love. My dad, the realist, always giving tough love, and my mom the big dreamer. It was a perfect match of equal balance that I have told them both; I would never change a thing. How we were raised, all fighting together for each other's dreams, and bringing the most out of the life we were given.

My parents were high school sweethearts, we all should be so lucky but to make it how they did, and how others have before them. Marriages lasting 10, 20, 30, 50 years I applaud you. You give all of us hope, inspiration and joy towards what love should be.

Some of us take longer to find that or to find that perfect moment. Some of us let it pass by, but I ask you not to. Chase what your heart and mind tell you. To me, live each day with love, it's a chance but be strong. Strong enough to be turned down, brushed away but don't ever give up. It's like everything else, never stop till you get what you want out of life. Keep reaching.

Honestly, anything in life is this way, from what I've learned. Never give up on the life, the dreams you truly feel you deserve. If you don't know the skill to achieve it, learn the necessary skills or find the ones that do. But most importantly, love the journey, love meeting new people and taking on new challenges. Embrace the path that life turns you in the direction of your dreams. And if you wake up each morning believing in that dream, loving that dream throughout the day and going to bed with that dream at your pillow at night. Life will lead you in mysterious ways.

You may not believe it or see it at first. But take a step back, outside the box as if you were looking at a famlly member or friend. Giving 100% honest, loving advice. How would your thoughts and reasonings, feelings shape itself then? It should be different, from when you feel excitement or sadness...true emotion. Escape from that moment, and evaluate your life, the direction you wish to go as a project. Write it down, goals you wish to achieve and be specific. Giving dates and times, staying positive that no matter hardship, turn or fork in the road.... I will reach my dream.

Make an assessment of your life, start at the end. What do you want to accomplish before you die? Ask yourself, "I am I doing whatever it takes to get what I want?" "If you could do anything in the world and be successful. What would it be? What do you want to do everyday? This is your purpose. Do a list of things that bring you joy. Your heart, your life is your responsibility. Power is in taking responsibility and accessing your life.

Access what things you feel that are keeping you from what you truly want. On the left side of the paper write down your dreams and details that you truly want. On the right side, write down things that are keeping you from those dreams and wishes. Once you have your list write down on a separate sheet of paper, a plan of action to reach those dreams. Take your first paper, tear it in half and throw away the list keeping you from what you really want. Combine your two lists together and set goals on accomplishing everything that you want. Don't ever stop till you do.

Another great exercise is to place a small dot on a piece of paper. Close your eyes and breathe in deeply. Slowly and think about what you truly want, taking 5 to 10 minutes to truly think. Focus on those dreams in vivid detail as if you already have them. Now write down this list all around the dot on the paper. Once you have your list, place a circle around all the detailed items of your dreams and keep this on you. In your purse or wallet, always on you so you can constantly visualize your wants and desires. Stay positive in all your thinking when you look at these each day and believe you can have them. Focus on the dot as your dream, no matter how big or outrageous. Then when you close your eyes, breathe in slowly so that those large dreams are a small portion of this world. Believe you already have each and that they are achievable.

Because that is what life is, it's your own project. Your own perception of what life should be, so change it...if nothing else.... please chase it.

No matter who you may offend or hurt. Who may follow and who will be left behind. It's your life, and how you want to live it. Now within reason, but if those around you truly love you. They will either follow or support you, leave you behind or to be free....

Life, your heart....it should be free, always. I have had many in my life hinder me from the person I always felt I was. Who I was born to be. If that family member, friend or the love of your life can not understand your honesty, and who you feel you are deep down as a person. Talk to them and tell them from your heart this is what you want.

You need to be this way, or wear this, change this.... garbage. I'm asking you to be you, yourself, 100% authentically you. Life tends to reward

you for things you believe in, your passions, what you stand up and fight for. And what more to believe in, than yourself and your dreams.

At first, it will seem harsh, hard, scary and some may say riveting or fun. Who knows, we are all different, writing our own stories. Put on this planet in our own unique ways and paths in life. But you must learn to love yourself, your dreams before you can another. Trust me on this, no matter the hardships that come with life. If you fail this rule, you will never grow, move past the negative and achieve a beautiful life.

Isn't that what it's all about, loving one another, chasing and capturing dreams. And those who truly love and understand one another. Or love one enough but don't understand. They will seek the training and understanding to be alongside that person, nurture and develop that miracle. That dream will come true, keep fighting and in the end, the person not in front or behind you. But who stands beside you, always and truthfully will achieve their dreams. Your dreams and any dream beyond your wildest imagination you have ever thought of.

It's funny now, at the point of happiness in my life I have. I have not made any more money, had any miraculous change in relationship status. Quite the opposite, but I have finally let go of controlling life, but enjoying it. Noticing little things like a kid, meeting and talking to strangers to hear their story.

I've always had anxiety but wanted to meet new people I see every day. Hear their story, try to help, understand it, but ultimately learn from each experience. It's amazing when you choose to truly let go. "You're not a tree" as Jim Rohn the motivational speaker has famously said. Hint, anyone one who has never heard his speeches. Take the time, his outlook, and delivery on life. Absolute perfection. I try to start my day off daily listening to him first thing in the morning. "You hate your neighbors, job, surroundings, relationship…. change it."

Life and everything in it, when we look at the past. It's no longer in the moment. You may miss it, let the past and all your faults go. Start today, looking towards the future and where you truly want to go. You can start on a trip, but if you don't have a goal or end destination. How can we truly head where we want to go?

As Tony Robbins has said, "Imagine, if your beliefs guaranteed you can never get, to where you want to go." You have a destination that you want to achieve, and a start point. Now we may not know every twist and turn along the way, but we don't have to. We must focus on what we want, believe we can get there and know our ultimate goal, dreams and desires, is our destination. We can make it timeless in everything we do.

Below is a study of the human brain at Cambridge University.

C. Stanton

This is amazing. Try to read the paragraph below, then consider what it actually says. The mind is a beautiful, wonderful thing isn't it?

According to a rschearch at Cambridge University, it deosn't mttaer in waht oredr the ltteers in a wrod are, the olny iprmoetnt tihng is taht the frist and lsat ltteer be at the rghit pclae. The rset can be a total mses bcuseae the huamn mnid deos not raed ervey lteter by istlef, but the wrod as a wlohe and the biran fguiers it out aynawy. Wow

The human mind doesn't care the start or how you get there. Just that you have a start and an end goal. Your heart and dreams are the same way. It doesn't matter if you don't know exactly how to get where you are going or how to achieve your dreams. Just believe in them, your end result and your brain will figure out a way to get there.

"It doesn't mean pain and suffering won't come." "Whatever comes, look for the good in all things." "Don't stay in pain; life's too short." "Analyze and control what you can." Tony Robbins

Live each day, in the moment as if it was your last. Trust me, from a kid who has secretly battled anxiety, depression, to an adult. It never goes away, but you can make incredible shifts in your thinking starting today. Map your destinations and your dreams. Focus on the start, what do these events in my life truly mean, and how am I going to get to where I want to go. We don't have to always know each and every detail at the start and often times we don't. But just start, focus on what your dreams are telling you, believe that you can get there, and life will lead you in the direction you need to go.

Thinking of three things each morning to be truly grateful for. Family, friends, a job, a sunset, the flowers, nature, your pet, who knows an ice cream shop. Whatever brings you happiness start there. It doesn't have to always be huge things; I think the greatest things in life are often the small ones. Little moments that make the biggest impact on your heart and they are most often free.

Start now, do what's right for you and that's something I try to continue. It's not selfish, to think of yourself and what makes you happy. It's to help you grow, what makes you the happiest you possibly can be in life each day. Money is not everything; I believe experiences and the relationships you build every day are. It can take you to extraordinary paths and places.

In the Bible, birds are mentioned. Free flowing, fighting against the wind and with it. They soar carefree, not knowing when winter is coming, where their next meal will come from or having shelter from the elements. Trusting of the ways of the world, that all will be provided for them. If they don't like their surroundings, they fly to a new location. Every day presents them with new challenges but trusting that the world each day will provide what is needed. Life is what we make it and shape it to be.

Life I believe is like a caterpillar and once you're called to heaven, the afterlife, reincarnated whatever your beliefs, you shed the shell of this world. Any pain, any hurt, any wrong doing prior is wiped away if you believe in something. And a beautiful tranquil transformation is made into our new selves, for our new life…. Amongst Angels.

C. Stanton

Ch. 5. A House Full of Children

"What is a home without children? Quiet."

—Henry Youngman

"Each day of our lives, we make deposits in the memory banks of our children."

—Charles R. Swindoll

Life growing up I could not have asked for a more loving family. My dad worked in a factory, the same job he's had since graduating high school. My mom her position was of that, being a mom. My dad's side of the family, just 10 minutes north of Cincinnati, and my mom's parents. Five houses down on the left, on a quiet dead-end street in northern Kentucky.

My mother's dream house covered with trees in the front yard with plenty of open space. Before moving us from a suburb of Cincinnati, Norwood where my parents met in high school. We would take visits to see them. Sitting out on the covered side porch for breakfast. Toast with grape jam, pancakes, biscuits and gravy, grapefruit with the sugar rim topping with juice. And my mom always dreamed of raising kids up the road from her parents. Having a big enough yard for all her children and the neighborhood kids to play. One house always seemed to catch her eye, covered with a large trees in the front yard.

The older married couple who owned the home before, were secluded, kept to themselves and only talked to one man on the street named Leo. My grandfather Curtis Mobley who I look and resemble so much. He was the most loving, caring man I have ever known, and I try to embody his spirit every day.

He was friends with Leo and would talk to him to see if they ever would be remotely, interested one day in selling.

My family still talks of him all the time. Soft-spoken, loving and kind, he never knew a stranger. But when he said something, it had an impactful effect on other's lives. When he said something, it meant something.

An Air Force veteran, a Kentucky Colonel which I'm extremely proud of. It's amazing when you sit and think of how you are here. One chance meeting can change your life and everything you do. Who we meet, who we fall in love with. The jobs we take, the decisions we make every day all have impacts on where we're going. We all are very lucky if you look at the greater scheme of things.

So kindly with Leo introducing Curt to them, asking if they would ever think of selling this home to his daughter. She and her husband having two little boys and are wanting to get out of the city. They want to run and play sports, and this place would be perfect. Her husband Jeff is big into the outdoors and would have his own peaceful paradise with the woods out back. You would be helping a growing family, giving these kids room to breathe, play and grow. And so, it was as fate has it. They decided to sell to help a young family's dreams.

Angel Among Us

My parents would raise us all in this home on a dead-end quiet street. Welcoming my younger brother Adam and twin sisters along the way. Filled with laughter and many great memories, but not all life is pure joy, and this moment is one of them.

2007, on a Thursday I lost my mom it was beyond tragic. I don't know if any of you have ever lost anybody this way. With that sudden unexpected heart-wrenching feeling in your gut but that's got to be the worst type. The death, I've lost family members from cancer, heart attacks things like where they were sent to the hospital and they're just in pain, but you don't talk to your best friend the night before about dreams and wishes. And then lose her the next morning.

And at one point when I was living in Nashville pursuing my dream as a singer-songwriter, we thought that my mom's heart was not pumping at 50%. The heart specialists seeing her for the last couple years. At this point, everything was going great, and she was expected to make her last heart appointment that week. And then after that, they said everything would be good. But she seemed to have a cold for about 3 days. And it didn't seem to be anything more than just a sore throat.

Some health issues were present with my mom. My mom once got some money after a class action lawsuit that gave her sugar diabetes as well as some heart issues. She had anxiety, and depression that was at times mentally draining on her. Also, rhebotory arthritis did not help her as well, as she was constantly in pain taking medication to offer little to no relief. But I try to focus on the great memories, traditions and morals she enstilled in us all.

From that I remember watching my last movie with her which is my all-time favorite, Forrest Gump. With her, that was one of our special things we would share together. Watching movies, me and her we would stay up late at night enjoying some laughs together. I remember once watching Monty Python and the Holy Grail. Which I must admit, I'm not a fan of British comedy. But put Monty Python or Bennie Hill on, and I'll laugh with the best of them.

Late that night, having my grandmother coming out of her bedroom aggravated from being woke up from us making so much noise. And I'm sure we were a little loud laughing at the screen. Her feelings changed though, when she walked in, and she saw how happy I and her were. Watching some goofy movie from the 70's cracking up. If you have never had the opportunity to have seen it and you like Medieval Times, King Arthur history with a very funny take. I highly recommend you take the time to enjoy this hilarious classic.

But from that the last movie I get to watch with her and if you ever notice on Mother's Day. It doesn't matter what part of the country I'm in the movie Forrest Gump always plays. The first Mother's Day without her and I didn't really catch it till after she passed. But it's got some great symbolism about life. How to treat others, some amazing lines in the script and everything on how you should treat yourself and other human beings. Not to mention the bond between a mother and her son.

I didn't catch it till 3 years later at the end of Forrest Gump there was a scene where Forrest finally gets one of his dreams. He finally gets his Jenny. And no matter what he's always loved her. He never judged her and that's how we all should treat each other. Because you never know what people are going through. You never know what things outside of what they're doing, outside of our what, what they're truly dealing with in life.

He fights for what he loves, chasing his dreams and through all hardships never giving up. Thru war, hardships of being a shrimp boat Captain every challenge life threw at him, never stopping. And Jenny was his ultimate goal, his ultimate love and he never lost sight of her. No matter what part of the world he was in, what hardship and dangers he faced, he thought of his mom, but mostly her.

One of the great scenes from the movie, her and Forrest talking as she lays in bed. "Forrest, were you scared over in Vietnam?" Forrest responds "Yes, well I…. I don't know. Sometimes it would stop raining long enough for the stars to come out. Then it was nice. It was like just before the sun goes to bed down on the bayou. Throws on a million sparkles on the water. Like that mountain lake, it was so clear Jenny it looked like there were two skies. One on top of the other. Then the desert when the sun comes up, I couldn't tell where Heaven stopped, and the Earth began. So beautiful." Jenny responds, "I wish I could have been there with you." Forrest looking at the love of his wife and giving a perfect response from the heart, "You were." He finally gets his Jenny marries her and then she dies from an unexpected illness. Such a special movie about dreams, love and the heart, never giving up. But also, for the one I and my mom share a special moment and bond with. I do not take this memory lightly and am thankful every day to have shared this moment with your mom. I'll never forget.

From there is the final scene at the end of the movie where Forrest is letting young Forrest off for the bus. He's making breakfast, he's hanging out with him, and that's all he cares about is loving this child. And at the end, if you remember there was a portion where there is a white feather at his feet, sitting on a stump at the bus stop. And then the exit music hits, and it blows up in the wind and then comes in front of the camera etc. etc. "Maybe we are just blowing accidentally in the wind." "Maybe we are just all accidentally connected or maybe it's not an accident at all."

What I didn't know, and I guess that's another reason I don't own the movie, but I hold it dear to my heart. Because I find it extra special that no matter where I am in the world, it doesn't matter, it always finds me. But I always feel like my mom is there. That she's still there watching it with me and I guess it's another one of our special things we share together.

And this is kind of why I'm writing this book. Because I know for a fact that she is still here and I want you to know. Your loved ones are as well, they are still with you, if you truly believe in your heart they are still with you, always. There is something that she said to me that registers with me, that will always stay with me. Sitting at my grandmother's dining room table as she got up, to walk towards the kitchen. "What do you think that feather represents?" One of the last things she said to me before going to her room and laying down for the last time.

And I said, "I really don't know Mom what do you think it represents" and from there she said, "Do you think it's Jenny, still around, you just can't see her?" "Letting Forrest know that she's still here, still around." Thinking now writing this, I am not even sure I've shared these memories with my family. I may have brought it up in times remembering her, but I doubt I have ever shared the detail, like I have with you in this book. Moments are so special no matter how small you may or may not think they are. But if it moves you and touches your heart, it will always make an impression on you, your soul and more than likely at least one other person. Life is about moving beyond yourself worth, your needs, growing, moving forward to help others.

But what I didn't know is how this moment would change me, and shape me into the thinking, and beliefs of today. I did not in this moment know that this was the start of the beginning, of the our last conversation. The last that we would share in this physical world as we know it. Also, as years passed, I started to catch little moments in the movie involving birds, and Jenny's thoughts on life.

Throughout countless times in the movie, even in some of Jenny's darkest moments. The bird symbolism pops up throughout the film. The feather, birds flying over Forest at her grave and he takes a moment to notice them. Even when Jenny is out in LA and is contemplating a leap from a high rise building. She wants to escape her pain and fly away like a bird. When she is a little girl hiding with Forrest in the back corn fields behind her house from her abusive alcoholic father.

"Pray with me Forrest, pray with me." "Dear God, make me a bird. So, I can fly far, far away from here." "Dear God, make me a bird. So, I can fly far, far away from here." Repeated over and over unfortunately not receiving her answer in the present moment the way she wished.

But life does not and most often doesn't reveal its answers. Doesn't deliver your hopes and desires in the first moment when you ask. But if you're deliberate in your thinking, shifting your thoughts towards what you truly want. Life at the perfect moment will reveal its gifts to you.

As we continued to talk as we normally did at night, about hopes and dreams. After asking me about the feather in the living room, sitting at the dining room table, we kept talking. But before she went to lay down to sleep, we went out on my grandmother's porch watching my little niece Ashlee play in the yard. One of her greatest joys, being a grandmother herself and spoiling that little munchkin all her days.

Buying her a swing set so she could play and enjoy being outside when she comes over to visit. Along with a canopy swing so she could sit many days with her and talk about Ashlee. Little munchkins busy day of Dora the Explorer or coloring in one of her many coloring books.

Sitting out on the covered porch, we continued to talk about life, dreams, and ambitions. I promised her I'd find my dream home one day; a Log Cabin wrap around porch and no neighbors. This is a dream I've always had as a kid growing up. Having horses and living out in peaceful nature. We talked more and describing as if we were painting a vivid picture. She had this idea to have one great dining room, with one particular feature.

To have a large table, so big that you would never be able to remove it from the room. Having to build the walls up around it, that if you ever wanted to remove it, you would have to cut it up in sections. One so large that at thanksgivings and Christmas all of the family could sit at one table, looking out at nature through the windows. Taking in the snow and the pines.

We also talked about an idea she had in investing in a local drive-in theater. My mom being a mom, so giving and good-hearted as she was, wanted to help in a struggling drive-in on the outskirts of town. One we spent at least one summer night together as a family. Taking in a couple of movies, in lawn chairs sitting around together with throw blankets under the stars with the smell of popcorn in the air.

Months before she seen on tv a commercial for a class action lawsuit, that a medication she was taking for years for pain was one that was mentioned. Which lead to sugar diabetes and other related health issues. Talking with my grandmother and myself asking if she should call. We said of course, take the chance what would it hurt. My dad though, being the realist said it will never happen, you're wasting your time. But the truth is, she wasn't. She didn't ask for this nor asked to have diabetes. Case in point, fight for what your heart tells you, no matter who says any different. Sorry, dad. ☹

But it's true, fight for equality, fight for your beliefs even if they are indifferent. What your passionate about, in the end, if we show no hate, only love. We all grow and learn from one another making the world a better place.

I didn't want her to use her money from the lawsuit on a drive-in theater; it wasn't that I didn't believe in it or what they are doing there. But I wanted her to enjoy it herself, and I knew I could give her that same experience in her own setting and eventually one day she would have it. One day I would find this amazing property and build it with my own two hands for all of us to enjoy. I've worked in IT for years and have constructed some large audio visual projects in my day. So, we talked the rest of the night about what we would do once it was done, and how much everyone would enjoy it.

The drive-in is something we do as a family at least once a summer. It brings back memories of being a kid, camping at gorgeous Laurel lake. Going into town to the Root beer stand for footlong cheese coney's and a float. It is now a tradition my brothers and sisters do with their kids now.

At the time, I didn't know this was the last time I would get to have with her. A heart to heart about life, dreams and goals. But she still speaks to us kids in other ways.

It's amazing to think how she helped me find this property we talked about and unfortunately the person I was with at the time, I lost it. But it led me to write this book to show love. To give back, turn a negative no matter how bad your story is, into a positive to help others. To learn some valuable lessons in life. That a house, a property, a car, all these things are just that, things. Materials that in the greater scheme of things throughout life, really mean very little. And that just shows the heart that my mom has, how she's able to still reach her kids even after death. Her heart and her passion for chasing dreams no matter how big or impossible they may seem. I like to think she has passed it down to all of us kids, sharing her heart to the next generation.

I want to thank you every day for the amazing person you were and still are, but I want to also thank my brothers and sisters. My dad as well, you shaped me to be the best I can be. To chase dreams and know I always have your full support.

My mom was always fighting thru anxiety and was always worried about her kids and worried about life. She would express it through words, through poetry, through art and handwritten cards. I could not love her enough and thank her. She's passed this down to all of us and she's helping to share this story to other people. I just love her so much and have been very blessed to share this story, experiences and my family with all of you.

She was my best friend, and she still lives through this book. I hope those that are kind enough to take the time to read with an open mind. You see that there's something beyond this. There's something beyond what we know, what we can see or understand. It's all about love, the heart and what we feel. Hopes, dreams and wishes. I thankful to share this with you and I'm blessed every day to be here to share this story with those who will listen.

But from the Forrest Gump movie, I'm seeing that feather for what it is. That we're only here for a short time, that this life we live, it's momentary and the legacy, the love we leave behind is what carries on. It's the impressions we make on people's lives that matter the most. The ones we leave behind, it's signs in little things that no one else would even know or pick up on. The character we leave behind and memories in our loved one's hearts is what makes the biggest difference. Finding our purpose and using that for the greater good. Using our talents for something larger than yourself. That's true purpose.

It's little things, personal clues and signals that they let you know, "hey I'm okay I'm up here in heaven. I'm not hurting anymore I just want you to know I'm loved and I'm okay." And with my mom, it's her signs or clues. Hers are the color purple, purple flowers, a random warm breeze and butterflies.

C. Stanton

Ch. 6. One of the Hardest Things

"Every day stand guard at the door of your mind."

—Jim Rohn

One of the hardest things I've ever had to do was I always used to sneak me and my mom Donato's Pizza. Founder's thin crust being our favorite, pepperoni sausage, banana peppers, ham and the occasional added onions, delicious. This was before Netflix, back when Blockbuster ruled the movie rental realm of the world. I used to sneak me, and her movies and pizza so we could spend the day together. This was my routine just about every couple days after I returned home from my stint in Nashville trying to make it in music. It's weird, for some reason she could tell I wasn't happy there being away from home. Things were not going as planned and it seemed like everything kept pointing me back home.

So, I did, and at the time I didn't quite understand all of my hardships and unfortunate bad luck. The harder I tried to fight for my musical career, controlling everything, the harder life stood up and said no. At this moment it's not meant to be, this is not your path. But life works in mysterious ways, and no fame or money would ever take the place of the six months that I got to spend with my mom before she passed. I cherished that time, not knowing what pain was to come shortly after my return back home.

But Thursday, June 14th, 2007 was a little different I couldn't sleep that night. My sisters, and mom were getting ready to take my dad for their wedding anniversary trip to Myrtle Beach in their last vacation together. It is a special place for them, where they spent their honeymoon together. And later with the help of my grandmother, bringing us years later to see the ocean for the first time as a family.

They wanted to take my younger sisters on this trip, before they went on to start their own lives. Full of college courses, studying and later a family of their own. They wanted to spend one last great vacation with them, but it was not meant to be.

I tossed and turned all night and into the morning, for some reason I could not sleep at all that night. I have never done this before, but something told me to look at old pictures when we all were kids. And the first photo album I got to was just of that. Our first trip to see the ocean, none of us kids have ever been to the beach, and my grandmother had promised my grandfather Curt. Papaw is what we called him, that before he passed from pancreatic cancer that my grandma would take us to see the ocean and fulfill a promise he wished he could have.

When he was stationed in the Air Force in Texas and saw the huge body of water for the first time, with what seemed to have no end. He thought it was one of the most amazing, relaxing and beautiful sights on the planet. I guess that's why my mom loved the ocean so much, that a part of her felt closer to her dad. And I guess a part of me, always feels closer to her when I see it. Listening to the waves crashing against the shore, and the light breeze coming off the water.

We always took camping vacations to beautiful Laurel Lake and with that comes plenty of wonderful memories. That's one thing with my mom she always was taking tons of pictures. In the day she passed away I couldn't thank her enough. Because we can remember so many good times that we forgot as life goes on, and I was looking through old photos. A lot of times we really hated standing around and posing for so many. But mom I want to thank you for taking in the moment and capturing those amazing memories for us all. We gave you a hard time in those moments, but now we all appreciate it. Mom, thank you.

Those of us all together, sun in our eyes at Myrtle Beach, happy times. For the first time seeing the ocean, it was an amazing, peaceful sight. My grandfather Curt whom I look so much alike, when he passed away from pancreatic cancer in 1988. That's the first time I experienced death was with him, and it was very rough on us all. He was my hero and still is one of the most caring, amazing person's that I have ever known. People still talk of him and of how loving he was towards everyone he ever met.

He wanted my grandmother to promise that she would take us to see the ocean. "Those boys and little twins need to see it." And as we stood there all together as a family, sun in our eyes taking our first photo with the ocean in the background. We all shed a few tears, looking out over the water thinking of him. My grandmother Shelby. She gave us that gift when I was 13 and fulfilled a promise. I can't thank her enough.

On that Thursday I called down to my grandmothers a couple of times and I never got an answer. So, I laid down at 10 in the morning after looking through old photos, laughing and smiling before closing my eyes for roughly a half hour. Just laughing at some of the funny pictures and memories from our first trip to see the ocean together in Myrtle Beach. I don't even remember shutting my eyes and dozing off, but I must have for few minutes. Then I heard a banging on the door and the world's most gut-wrenching scream I've ever heard in my life, and it's still haunts me today.

I enjoy Halloween it's my favorite holiday, my favorite time of year with the leaves changing, the air so crisp and clean. You can dress up to be whatever you want. But that scream it still gives me chills today and I can hear it in my head when I think back. It was my sister Autumn. and it takes you back to that point in time and all the hurt in that moment.

At this time my grandmother was sick with pneumonia, fresh out of the hospital three days earlier. And I just spoke to my mom the night before out on the carport. Told her I loved her, gave her a big hug before she went back to her room and laid down to go to bed for the night. When I came to the door, my sister said something, tears in her eyes. It didn't register; it took me two times before my brain would even compute it. I could not control her, but I finally grabbed her in the middle of the street. She fell to the ground and she said it for the third time as I try to pick her up in my arms. As I'm holding her sobbing uncontrollably for the third time, those three words did. "Mom is dead; Mom is dead!"

Separated as hearing that my grandma had just passed away from pneumonia. I think it's just a blocker your brain does in moments so hurtful and shocking as these. It keeps working, but when hurt so severely, it blocks out the pain. It's a barrier, a fog that for months I can't remember much of anything.

We live on an older street in northern Kentucky that a lot of the people there are retired. It's an older community, and everybody knows everybody. The neighbor across the street rushes out to ask me what is going on, and if she's okay. After she said the third time, she was in shock and didn't know what to do with herself knowing who my mom was. Thinking of her heart and how great a person she was so true to the love of giving and life.

I just remembered the neighbor crossing the street as my sister Autumn is in so much pain. Asking "What is wrong, is everything ok?" Laying in the street, catching her as she crumbled to the ground. "Mom's dead, mom's dead." Gravity takes over falling in shock, but I remember her jaw dropping and placing her hands over her mouth looking at me. She started to cry uncontrollably with my sister. Leaning down on my right knee. I was just in protective mode at this point, unsure of what else to do.

Then as I reached down, Autumn wrapping her arms around my neck, burying her face in tears into my neck and chest. The tears herself she couldn't control and cried right there alongside my sister in the street. "Oh my God, I don't know what to say. Are you ok?" I said, "yes, we will be ok, we will be ok. I need to get her down the street, calm her down and in bed". And I did, as I carried my sister sadly down the street not knowing what to expect or what to do. Life felt like it was moving in slow motion, as I tried to be strong and help her any way I could. My grandmother, not knowing exactly what to do. All these thoughts racing through my head but at the same time, in a fog, blank.

At this point something in our mind's triggers, we may be truly stronger than we may even imagine. I said to myself, trying to stay strong. "I must fix this." But there is no fixing here; there is no going back, not with a life-altering moment as this. I have to get my sister down the street and keep her calm as she kept balling her eyes out in uncontrollable pain.

I just keep remembering the moment picking her up out of the road, and I remember telling myself in my head. Stay strong for her, my mom and my family. Not fully registering yet that it was my mom was the one who had passed. I didn't want to believe it, not one notion of the fact that this could ever be true. My sister, I feel for her still as she was the one who found her in her room. Lying motionless in her bed, with a movie in her tv player. Being that of The Father of the Bride with Steve Martin, undoubtedly watching it the night before thinking of my younger brother Adam's ensuing wedding to occur in 29 days. My sister Autumn, her background being a nurse, she tried to perform CPR, but it was already too late, she was already gone.

I was in total shock, and my eyes started to well with tears. I fought them back, telling neighbors that we were fine repeatedly. Although, we both knew we were not. I carried her down the street in a haze.

Once I got to my grandmothers, struggling to open the front glass door with Autumn in my arms. And once inside I put her in her bed, asking her to try and get some sleep. Giving her some water and some anxiety medication, my grandmother had to calm her. My grandmother sitting in the living room on oxygen, with her hands over her face, shaking her head. "No....no.... no.... no.... no... no.... Sandra.... no.... no.... no".... repeatedly over and over.

And all I can think about is call your dad, call your brothers and to call your sister Amber as they are all at work. Tell them to get home safely, just come home from work, it's a family emergency and I'll explain it when they get to grandmas. Work will understand.

It's hard reliving this part of the story and even telling it now. How you go to block out painful portions of your life, cut out those chapters woven in it and putting those memories in the back of your mind. Reliving them on paper. Details lost seem to creep back through the pages, quietly back in writing this tale for the first time. I called them all and tried to calmly convey and have them understand something horrible has just happened. Trying to keep a collective head over it all, so they did not race home erratically to what was about to shock their whole world. I hope I never have to do this again in my life, but I just wanted to be strong for them and for my mom.

Everyone asks, "Is it grandma?" I said "no." Just as I first thought, "was its Grandma?" I just held on to hope that I could get through this day, to get them all here safe without worry. I can say after talking with everybody they all asked if it was her again, and I repeated with a blank "no." "Just get home to grandma's, and I'll tell you when you get here." Like how I thought with Grandma just getting out of the hospital. As they all kept asking, my only response was "no, just get home and I'll tell you when you get here." "Something bad has happened" and just being strong for them and my mom.

It was weird, when I tried to call my dad on his cell phone a few times, he didn't answer but he works in a busy factory. The same job he's had his whole life, so I had to end up calling the company number. Which they directed me to his department and connected us by paging me through.

They were High School sweethearts and they raised the most amazing family ever. I wouldn't trade anything in the world for that. All the struggles, the highs, and lows. They achieved the ultimate dream as parents. Raising a healthy family, giving them all the love and opportunities to chase each other's dreams. No amount of fame or money could ever replace the accomplishments that they have done. What we all went through I would change nothing, they made us who we are today and I'm so proud of my family.

But when I called my dad at work, he knew right away. It caught me completely off guard, but I wouldn't confirm or tell him the truth as he asked and knew. I just didn't have the strength to let him know over the phone. I just couldn't do it. That connection I guess, sometimes you just know. When a piece of you, your heart is gone, you just know.

Having to call my family, call my best friend to let him know. That my mom has passed even looking back now. It's bittersweet because she went in her sleep, we all should wish that. No pain, no struggle just one day you go to rest and the next your waking up where the creation of all things has begun. You're where at this moment, where you're supposed to be.

Thinking of her and trying to be strong for everyone at this time. Shock and disbelief helped I'm sure in the numb crushing feelings I was sharing.

My brother Shane was the first to get there and then Adam, Amber and finally my dad. I came up to Shane, with Grandma in the back ground. Giving him a hug and with that, him seeing her in the living room. In his mind he knew then, with anger and shock in his eyes, I held him. Then letting out a couple of tears, he went over to Grandma on the couch. "No…Sandra….no….no…no…"

Then Adam, Amber and lastly my dad Jeff. I was a zombie at this point; everything was a haze as they came in one by one. Seeing grandma there, hearing Autumn in the back bedroom crying uncontrollably. Moments like these can only be explained as gut-wrenching, horrible, life changing.

The ambulance had shown up at this point, yellow and red piercing lights rearing its ugly head, thru the front living room window. Neighbors gathering outside on the street, and the paramedics coming in the front door. My brothers and I step out into the front yard to try and get some fresh air. My dad stayed with my grandmother to answer questions, as my sister Amber tended to her twin, Autumn in the back bedroom.

All three of us out front by a maple tree that was planted out by the street, by our grandfather Curt. We stood there in shock, saying little to nothing. Nothing needed to be said, wiping tears away with the blank stares, staring at the side of the ambulance. Then the paramedics a few moments later appeared out from the corner of the house. Pulling a sheet covered gurney to the bumper of the truck to load it in the back. As they did, muttering "Sorry for your loss" as they quickly sped up the street.

More tears fell as my brothers, and I hugged out at the road. Wiping tears, a deep breath and tilting our heads to the sky. A few neighbors asked what was going on, inquiring about my grandmother. Which we said "No." Fighting back the tears together, "it's our mom." As they gasp, the same as the neighbor up the street did prior.

Walking in the front door in a fog, to rejoin my father and grandmother in the living room. My dad glancing over some paper work just handed to him at the dining room table. Amber emerging from the back bedroom, tears in her eyes, hugged us all, then my dad. Moving on to grandma, with her oxygen. Leaning back on the couch with her hands on her knees, arms outstretched. Trying to take a deep breath, her head leaned back. Trying to deal with the life, that was her daughters, forever changed.

I tried to still focus for my family on all the great things she accomplished in life and for us kids. She was amazing, and the most caring person on the planet. She loves us all so much; I know this was by no means her plan to leave this world, her family behind at 51. But life sometimes does not work out the way we plan; we often don't understand the meaning behind it. And this was definitely one of those times.

My dad proceeded to get up from the dining room table, into the kitchen towards the basement door. We all asked if he was alright, as he turned the handle to the door fighting back the tears. "Yes, I'm ok." Knowing good and damn well he wasn't, who would be. As I followed him down the stairs to grab some photo albums for everyone.

She looked so peaceful when I saw her down there in her room, lying in her bed. It shocked me at first as the ambulance showed up and then had gone. I had thought while whole time, they had taken her to the funeral home. I went downstairs to gather some photo albums that she cherished so dearly. And there she was, asleep lying on her right shoulder to the left of the bed. Books on the floor, and pictures. A picture of my little niece, her little munchkin on the end table near her.

Angel Among Us

Sitting in her little pink rocking chair, smiling showing off her little dimples, brown curls and yellow sundress.

That's when I saw my mom in the past tense and tears fell for the first time. I said, "Dad, let's go, I don't want to see her like this." And he said, "you go, give me some time with her." So, grabbing an arm full of photo albums, and walking upstairs to the living room. I laid them out on the floor of the living room as my family gathered, opening the first one. A picture of my mom, I never recalled seeing before.

I remember the view, as it was from my parent's old home in Cincinnati. Norwood a suburb just north of downtown, the house I was born in. She was in her white wedding dress on the day my parents got married. It's actually one that my sister Amber receives compliments on all the time tattooed on her back shoulder in honor of her.

She was sitting on a front porch swing as she often did, in her white wedding gown. But I'm not sure if it's from the picture being aged or the material used back then in the early 70's. But she has an aura, a glow about her in this picture. No feelings of hurt or pain, all joy looking like an angel. Ready to be a wife and to start a family of her own.

That's how I want to remember her, and what I focused on at this time with my family. Anyone at this moment, would have nothing but hurt. And you can do nothing but focus on the pain. But I tried to look at the positive, if any at this time and believe me it was truly difficult. We told funny stories and we all began to focus on the great times instead of the present hell we found ourselves in.

My brother Shane God bless him, he still beats himself up about not saying anything to my mom, saying goodbye, good night. Seeing her early that morning as she usually went to the refrigerator for a late-night snack. I just want you to know, that its ok. There is no way you could have known, just as we all didn't. One thing we carry in our hearts, she truly is with us always, no longer in any pain, any hurt or any sadness.

We continued telling funny stories, sharing great memories as a family. Even sharing some laughs but one amazing thing I pointed out as we were gathered around. Look at the last week, all the crazy amazing things Mom talked about doing for so long, for years.

Painting Amber's room is the one that sticks out in my mind. Her favorite color, orange. Taking the time to make so many things perfect that week and complete. Pampering herself, putting on makeup, a new dress and having her hair done. She always put her family first, and never spoiled herself. But for once she did, and she was truly happy all week. Excited for the upcoming vacation, the upcoming wedding and soon to be new adventures. Excited about her youngest son Adam, following her and Jeff in their footsteps marrying his high school sweetheart.

And maybe that's exactly what it was, the gift we were given thru her. For all her struggles, the wreck she had my first day of my 8th-grade year that almost killed her. Flipping her car multiple times, working a 3rd shift job to help us get by. And not knowing where she was for a day. Her purse, ID thrown from the car and air lifted to university hospital. A Jane Doe, and all the mental challenges she faced going through that.

Then the month leading up to her passing. Doing things, she talked about for years, and completing them one at a time. I couldn't be more thankful, that thru it all she was the ultimate mother to us. Granted the grace and dignity to dream as she always did in this life. Pushing all her kids to never stop dreaming for what their heart truly wants and deserves. Sleeping peacefully in her bed, in no more pain, no more hurt, only happiness. An endless vacation. I miss you mom....

We all do.

C. Stanton

Ch. 7. Visions

"Vision is the art of seeing what is invisible to others."

—Jonathan Swift

"The future belongs to those who believe in the beauty of their dreams."

—Eleanor Roosevelt

So, 3 months have past since losing my mom, and I was working out of town on a project in Springfield Ohio. The largest High School in the state of Ohio at the time. Working 4 10 hour days with a nice 3-day weekend. But for some reason this Thursday I got home 3 o'clock in the afternoon. I'm just feeling tired and thinking about her. It just felt different, and I called my friend Brian just to let him know I was back in town. Wanting to hang out, I just told him I was going to lay down for a little bit and take a nap. With me, I've always had issues remembering dreams, have my whole life where I only remember 1 to 2 a year. And for the ones that I do they always seem to come true like Deja vu. I remember just feeling super tired all of a sudden, calling him on the last bit of the drive home.

And once I got home, I could not close my eyes quick enough. It was like I was in a deep sleep; a trance of sorts and it was almost as if I was recalling a memory. Closing my eyes to darkness, rolling them to the back part of my head, and thinking of her. Forcing my consciousness to a dream state, breathing slowly relaxed almost in a hypnotized state. It was so vivid I've never had a dream like this in my life.

It was like a vision, and I remember walking up my grandmother's basement steps, coming up to her door that led into the kitchen. Every detail, so vivid. I could see and smell the food on stove. I could see a ham and turkey, fresh from the oven on top of the stove. Mashed potatoes, green beans, and fresh dinner rolls that I could smell thru out the whole kitchen.

My first thought was this must be a memory of Thanksgiving or Christmas as we would always spend it down the street at my grandmother's house together as a family. I can hear other people in the background. My little niece laughing, and it sounded like she was running through the halls. I can hear my two brothers Shane and Adam as it sounded like they were in a back bedroom playing video games, probably Halo at the time. My grandmother was in the kitchen as well as her sister Beulah. Along with her daughter Patty who is my cousin, but we always called her Aunt Patty. Being close in age to my mom and that she was one of my mom's closest friends.

I go to turn to my left to walk out of the kitchen into the dining room and living room area searching for Ashlee no doubt. I could hear that little munchkin laughing and running in the back hallway. But when I come around at the doorway, I met my mom. It shocked me to my every being, my core and she was wearing this purple dress. The one she wore the night I surprised her for a dinner date and a movie. As this again is the color purple coming back into my life.

But also, it meant something more. A few months prior I had this idea of taking my mom and grandmother out for dinner and a movie. I walked in, dressed up. Ready to go out, after flying in from work from some far away town. I had this idea as I do to surprise people and to do something out of the ordinary and nice, just because.

The first thing when I walked in the front door to my grandmother's house, my mom asked is "who is the lucky lady tonight?" And I said, "you two." I just remember the big smile on her face. But my grandmother just wanted me to spend time with my mom. "You two go and spend it with each other." I tried to convince her but she said; "no you two go out and have fun, I'll be fine."

So, she took a little time to put her makeup on and a beautiful purple dress she just got. The one she eventually was laid to rest in. It was beautiful, with different purple colors shimmering from it, it made her feel amazing, like a million bucks. And undoubtedly made me smile all night long spending this much needed time together, just the two of us.

We went down to Newport on the Levee which is right on the Kentucky side on the Ohio River overlooking downtown Cincinnati. We spent the whole day together going to Johnny Rockets for dinner having a couple of burgers and some milkshakes. Deciding on seeing The Prestige at the movie theater. One of the great memories from my mom and our movie collection. Christian Bale and Hugh Jackman portray two master magicians in the early part of the century, competing for legitimacy and worldwide fame.

Remembering this night out, also reminded me of a time when I tricked my parents into going on a date together. I called my grandmother's house to tell my mom I was coming home. And for her to get ready and that I was going to take her out to eat. After getting off the phone with her, I immediately called my dad. And said, "hey dad I'm almost home for the week and wanted to see if you wanted to meet me for dinner." Which my mom felt like having a strawberry daiquiri, so we decided to go to the local Applebees in town.

I can still remember it seeing the look on my dad's face. Shock, then a smile and laughter as he walked in the door. My mom soon had that same look as he came to the table to sit for dinner. Such a great day as well, laughing enjoying our time together. Talking about family, upcoming events, just spending moments together. What life is truly about, weaving moments together in time.

But in this dream, it was so vivid, so clear, so real, so true. I gave her a hug and could feel her. I could smell her perfume. She always wore lavender, and when I hugged her, I could smell the lavender. I started to think that this was a memory from a past family gathering. But it was so vivid and real. I have never had a dream like this before or one since. Especially one that I could ever recall a smell, let alone being able to feel, a hug with her arms wrapped around me and her head against my chest.

I started to talk with my mom about us all and small chit chat about what we were having for dinner. And where that little munchkin Ashlee was running through the house. And she responded clearly, which I found odd.

Any dream I ever had prior, were never this detailed not even close. Being able to clearly talk, ask questions and receive a clear response. It's usually garbled up in conversation, if you even get to the point of talking at all. I thought what if this wasn't a dream, what if it was a vision. That she was visiting me as I slept.

So, I started asking her questions on things that had happened after that terrible Thursday in June. Things, if this was me recalling a memory she would not be able to know or answer. My younger brother Adam and his high school sweetheart Jessica were set to be married just 29 days after my mom's passing. She was so excited for them both, happy and ready for them to start a life together as she did with her own.

They thought about putting it off, but thru family and conversations with others, they moved forward with it as they should. And I know my mom would have wanted them to do so as well. I asked about their wedding and if she knew about it. She said she did and that "it was beautiful." I asked her if she knew I was going to start my own cabling company. She said she did and that she was proud of me for trying. She always believed I could do it on my own better than the companies I previously worked for.

I asked if she was okay, if everything was alright. And she said, "yes, should be spending time with her dad." "Having fun, spending the days with him and family." And that's when I was thrown off; I'm starting to get upset realizing that we were no longer talking about the current. Things that happened after she passed away and there's no way that this could be a memory I was recalling in my dreams. Her responses were quick and straight from the heart. Smiling the whole time, with no feeling of hurt or pain in her face and eyes.

With this is when I awoke, tears in eyes and I remember looking at my alarm clock and it was 3:14. 14 minutes had transpired from the time I first fell asleep and when I awoke. Now the number fourteen is significant as my mom passed away three months prior on the 14th of June. I immediately went down the street to talk to my grandmother, wiping tears from my eyes as I walked down the street to her house. Ready to share about what just happened and described it to her. She listened intently and held my hand from her recliner as I sat on the couch across from her. Now she had me write everything down on a piece of notebook paper which is still in her bedroom.

Now after I did this I wrote everything down in descriptive detail, she went into her room and brought out other pieces of notebook paper. That apparently weeks leading up and even weeks after my brothers and sisters all had the same kind of experience with my mom visiting them in their dreams.

What a beautiful gift that was given. I felt like I got to spend 14 more amazing, wonderful minutes with my mom. A part of me didn't want to wake up, didn't want to leave. But after talking with her, hearing that she was ok and then becoming upset realizing that I was given this gift,

to spend one more moment with her. I felt like something was pushing me to go back, that it wasn't my time to stay. Needing to share these amazing experiences with others.

Now none of us knew this till my grandmother showed me. As I've heard of this before where people that have passed on will visit you in your dreams. And all us kids still felt like she was always around, we just couldn't see her, but we could feel her at certain times. Little clues or signals to let you know they're around. Me, my brothers and sisters always felt this way. And as a year moved steadily closer, after my mother's passing we always felt like a random warm breeze or a butterfly landing on your shoulder or finger was her saying "Hi." We always talked to my grandmother about this and somewhat with my dad each having our own separate experiences.

On the anniversary of her passing we all got together at my grandmother's house to cook a southern meal, things my mom enjoyed as a family. Lighting a candle in her honor placing it at the dinner table. We talked about funny stories and traditions, special things our family remembers about my mom. After this and getting ready to have dessert my grandmother reveals she has something for all of us.

We all don't know what to expect, but my dad had a hand in it as well. What we didn't know, is when my mom passed she left us all messages. Telling each one of her kids little messages to live by, one's we still have to this day. On the front of it was done in construction paper and had butterflies on it. We were all kind of shocked and didn't quite know what we were given or how to take it. All of us passing it around, reading out loud the notes from our mom. But the one that really hit home was the one for my sister Amber. "Amber take care of your sister always and whenever you feel a warm breeze or see a butterfly land on your shoulder or finger. That's me saying Hi."

We couldn't believe it. Absolutely in shock, looking at one another across the dining room table as we read thru each other's notes from our mom. Feeling her heart thru the pages of every word. Our thoughts on what we all felt for the past year, sensing she was near. She confirmed it in her own writing, messages for her children beyond this life and of what we know.

C. Stanton

Ch. 8. Taking a Leap

"In the end, we only regret the chances we didn't take."

—Anonymous

Years have passed after losing my mom, that moment of heartbreak and after meeting my wife in Cincinnati. I thought a part of that was filled; she was the most beautiful thing I've ever seen. She was down-to-earth, laid-back, not materialistic at all and It just worked till the day that we got married. We were fun and always kept it that way, well at least at first. A few months in, we just decided being happy to run off to Nashville to get married. Wild and carefree, telling only a handful of our plans. My best friend Brian was the only one in on it on my side, and not even my dad knew about our crazy plans.

We orchestrated a trip to Nashville, a town I love. We bought her wedding dress online making sure it fit correctly weeks in advance. But as the week closed in on the 10th of March, stress started to rise. As her dress had not arrived yet, just days before were scheduled to leave. And yet, not knowing if it was going to fit correctly or not.

Trying to keep her calm and staying positive that things typically tend to work out as they should. Luckily, she called me at work as she got it a couple of days before we were to leave. What a sigh of relief that was, as we only had a couple of days for her to try it on and get everything ready. Telling my dad of our plans to take a long weekend trip for the second weekend of March. Which was not a hard task at all. It was just going to be a fun weekend, but he loves Nashville, so it took little convincing.

So, she ended up finding a place called The Belmont mansion. An absolutely gorgeous place that host weddings and tours. Something that looked as if you stepped back in the time of Pride and Prejudice. The colors, history, and architecture was absolutely gorgeous and perfect, exactly what we needed. Very reasonable on the price, Pastor included as well as some unique photos and scenery that we would normally not get anywhere else. I'm traditional and somewhat old-fashioned in most of my ways, as I was even the day that we got married I did not want to see her in her dress.

I kept my eyes closed rummaging around in our hotel room to find her dress and to help zip it up. Before putting her in a luxury Taxi and sending her on her way. I wanted everything to be perfect and did not want any bad luck or superstitions to ruin it.

Now my dad is thinking that we are just going to a nice lunch or early dinner and that my ex-wife is not feeling well. Make sure you pack you know some slacks, nice shirt and tie. Telling him before we left, that on Saturday we plan on checking out this nice restaurant we heard about, just outside of downtown.

And then we get to the location just outside of Nashville, and my heart is pumping like crazy about ready to jump out of my chest. Meeting someone only a few short months later and then running off to get married but I did that. I would not recommend it but also, if your heart tells you to do something. You must follow it. Do it.

I thought this is it; this is the one person that I'm supposed to be with the rest of my life, she truly makes me so happy. I would do anything for this person, and no matter what crazy, randomness that ever came up. We embraced it and took it on as a team together, having fun along the way in our random adventures. Life throws you curves, and forks in the road. Take the time to enjoy these moments. Things are different with this girl yada, yada. The one thing I do recall, the one the most which stays in my mind. Is the moment when I first see her, when she walks down the stairs in her white wedding dress. It's like straight from a movie scene; it's how everybody should feel once you take that leap of marriage.

Time slows, and all things stop, everything cease to exist but these two hearts that are brought together, two become one. That's how I felt, and I did to the day I die. Looking back most people might think I'm crazy going through what I've been through, these experiences of life. What's greater than marriage, two people meeting by chance and a life collided, two hearts into one.

We all go into it thinking that it's going to work, and when it just doesn't, we fight for it and do some of the most ridiculous things imaginable to keep it. No one wants to fail in marriage or in love, but in the end, I want to look at it, I hope we both are better people from it. I like to think that I am and I'm hoping wherever she is in this world that the issues that we went through. The issues with herself, that she is a better person from it as well. I truly wish that from the bottom of my heart.

But in those moments before everything went down the crapper, I was in love. I have no doubt she was at one point, just the most amazing person when we met. Full of life, smiling and we always enjoyed life, having fun adventures together. Talking about dreams, about ambitions and one thing I noticed when I met her is all my dreams went on hold. My dreams became her dreams and I was okay with that. I wanted to give her everything she ever dreamed about no matter what it took. No matter how impossible or difficult, I wanted to give her everything.

And I felt that way, the moment we met. The moment when she walked into my heart and down those stairs. The red carpet on the steps, her white wedding dress, it was just a magical moment. But moments earlier seeing the look on my dad's face as we knocked on the front door.

Now, that was priceless. You see the plan was for the host to tell everyone who came to the door that we were here for the tour of the Belmont mansion. Then after words would be a nice lunch inside.

But when we knocked on the door, and I answered are you with the wedding party. I remember looking to my right, seeing the look on Brian's face waving his hands behind my dad. Then seeing the crazy, shocked look on my dad's face. Then a smile.

My friend Brian's face, red and a bit teed off, which honestly doesn't take too much to do. Sorry Brian but it's true, as I'm sure he would be quick to respond to this comment in his Jackie Gleason voice. "Yooou Summ B$tch!"

Looking back now it's kind of funny. They both were so shocked. One for my dad who had no idea that I was getting married today. And two for my buddy Brian that knew about it but was blown away when they revealed what was happening at the front door. Things were so carefully talked and planned out.

I and my wife went to the court house the day before to fill out the marriage license. Sneaking away briefly from them, telling my dad that we were going to head to the mall for a bit to go shopping. And we even had a great back story for him the next morning. One that she was feeling a little under the weather and wanted to rest while we were at lunch but would meet up with us later. It seemed like a great plan. But life often doesn't work that way. You can be meticulous in everything you do, and sometimes no matter what. Life will throw a wrench into your plans. Just embrace it and go along with the ride.

Brian quickly played it off and tried to convince her, "no we're here for the tour and luncheon." She would have nothing of it, taking no for an answer, "No you're here for the wedding at 12:30". Again, my dad

looking at me in shock but has now put it together that I'm about to get married in a few minutes and began to smile.

At this point there's no going back and "Pop's" well your apart of this crazy ride, enjoy it. But that moment when she's coming down the stairs, it was just like a movie. Time froze, it stood still, and everything is moving in slow motion. Everything and everyone in the room faded, and we were the only two people in it, and all I can do is smile. I finally found my angel, the one I've been searching for my whole life and at that moment I did.

From there we go thru the large double doors and walk up to the courtyard, gathered around with the pastor underneath a gazebo. As we said our vows to one another looking into each other's eyes. She had a unique look at things and wanted our wedding to be special. Writing our own vows to one another, and our commitment to our love, which was framed as a reminder in our home always. The ceremony was quick on a beautiful sunny day in Nashville which we were expected to get rain all day. But we lucked out, and it was bright, and the sunshine was out all day. Taking pictures having a wonderful time, around Music row and then from there, we were a couple; we were family.

At that time, I was still working for Tyco Integrated Security still one of the best jobs I ever had. Working for a financial firm installing DVR systems. Where just 12 years prior in Tampa covering the whole state of Florida for Fifth Third Banks. So, everything just seemed to fit, seemed to be coming together, full circle. Once we came back from our trip in Nashville telling my side of the family. Ashley's mother and father were the only one's on her side that knew of our plans to elope. But they could not have been happier.

My sisters and brothers were a little shocked, but I knew how I felt, I knew what I wanted, and she was the one. From this, we lived in a small house in Cincinnati that my grandfather owned. And it was just the three of us. My wife, myself and her dog Charlie. And life is good I just turned 32, but she felt like something was missing. One of the greatest gifts my ex ever gave to me was my dog Roo.

One of the things we talked about when we first started dating was my mom always wanted to have a miniature pinscher, and that was one of the things that my wife remembered. It was on my 32nd birthday she surprised me by finding one that was unique with a rare blue color name Roo. He was a rescue from a local shelter and had a skin rash on his back, unable to grow any hair. Keeping it covered with a blue bubble jacket he always wore.

I'm still so thankful that my ex remembered these talks. Talking with her in those early days and telling how I always wanted to get one of my own, for my mom. I just want to take this time and thank you for that. I love spending time with him as well as my other two pups. Charlie and Moose. But Roo Roo reminds me of my mom every time I see him, and always seems to bring a smile to my face.

Oh, married life, finding the girl I thought was the woman of my dreams. We didn't look back but taking a moment here it wasn't all bad and bat shit crazy. We did have some good times, great memories but things weren't as they seemed. But I won't focus on that as of right now. All I seen was a beautiful country bumpkin, everything I always hoped for in a wife. We worked as a team, focusing on goals to one day have a family, to have kids and to find our dream home.

Work and home life was going great, being 5 minutes from the house having a four-day work week helped tremendously, not to mention it was really nice. Having an extra day of freedom for newlyweds, traveling, chasing down dreams and making memories.

Roo he was a rescue like Charlie, and it was so funny I remember when we first brought him home. With his skin disorder on his back and the hair worn off, and he always wore sweaters is what the kennel told us. First, he was kind of shy and didn't know what to think of us or where he was at. But Charlie's quick to make friends and me and my wife sitting in the backyard watching them run and play in the yard.

We decided to get him used to having his coats and jackets off and got him some skin treatments to help with his back. A few days in and his rambunctious personality started to show, and you could tell he was happy to be here and around his new friend, his family. His back a grayish color from his shoulders tapering down to his back side on his body. After letting him outside, we started laughing hysterically to tears, as he looks like a little silverback gorilla running with his butt and back legs close to the ground as Charlie was chasing.

Married life was great; we would have dinner together have a small fire in our fire pit in the backyard making smores and life was good. I remember little things, looking back at moments seeing her looking thru the French doors smiling ear-to-ear the moment I got home. Her hair in the occasional pig tails, just being a family.

At the time she was working at a call center and absolutely hated her job, and I didn't want her to be sad or upset crying nightly. I was making enough money at the time, "Just quit if that's what you want to do." "And if it makes you happy, that's what makes me happy." Of all her dreams I want to do nothing more than to make hers come true. I just kind of stopped my own because I knew if I can make her happy, give her everything, that my dreams will come true as well.

Then the big "Uh Oh" moment. A couple of months in and she constantly in tears, upset. And then when I would ask "What's wrong?" she said that she was unhappy with her body. Which I'm confused with this, and not understanding at all, as she's beautiful just the way she is. Reluctantly I agree to go with her to her consultation. Meeting with one of the top plastic surgeons doctors in the Cincinnati area, after hearing everything they have to offer she decides to go forward with plastic surgery. Which I am totally against but if it would help her to feel better about her body, then that's what we'll do.

I decide to go along with it, and it was one of the worst decisions I ever could have made. She's looking to get breast augmentation which this is the first time that this was ever discussed just being 2 months into our marriage. Always crying when I would get home from work, we would sit down at dinner and talked for a couple of weeks before planning on what to do next.

Looking back now I wish I could have done more research and looked at more cases were mentally and physically cases not turning out good for the client and their loved ones. But her mind was made up, she wanted to feel more like a woman, eventually having the surgery but she went larger than what was initially discussed and what I was told.

So, the day of the surgery everything was peaceful and calm that morning. Both of us a little nervous but this is what she wanted. Once in the operating room, I waited reluctantly watching ESPN in the waiting room. She was still back there in the recovery room and 45 minutes to an hour goes by longer than she was supposed to get out. And the doctors and nurses were tell me she's doing fine, she's doing great but would not let me see her. I started to get really nervous and demanded to see her, to make sure that she was alright.

Obviously she wasn't and the first thing she said to me when she saw me was. "I want to punch you in the face." And it caught me off guard you, at first, I thought she was joking. Then I could tell in her eyes she was in severe pain. Her eyes welling up with tears, and I felt helpless. Like there was nothing I could do to help her, and it was scary. She was having a rough go with it, asking for pain medication right away, taking way longer than normal to awake in the recovery room.

I left the room and immediately spoke to the nurse. I'm like "what is going on, why is she in so much pain." In the consultation, we were told it would never be like this. Well in rare cases apparently this does happen, and the pain is quite traumatic. She happened to be the 1%, and I felt horrible. The last thing I ever wanted to do was hurt my wife, this was supposed to make her happy, not like this.

She was taking heavy doses of pain medication, and with her wanting to take them so often I was scared every day to leave her for work. That I would come home at lunch, that I was going to find her overdosed, lying motionless on the floor or in our bed. But I felt bad she was in so much pain. Bringing her food and ice, anything to get thru this pain. She was bed ridden for almost two months after and could hardly move.

But eventually she recovered from it, the pain slowly began to ease. From this moment the wheels started coming off, personalities changes from when we first met. Things she was totally against, spending money, not going to church, not listening to country music, the way she would dress even changed and so on. And then all sudden she started having issues with her mother constantly fighting bickering, yelling screaming over nothing for no apparent reason. Then came the question that she wanted to move to another town that maybe that was going to solve her issues.

It didn't, but I was willing to try anything, to make her happy again, to see her smile and enjoying life once again. And that's when I began to look for a new opportunity with work, which landed me in Louisville Kentucky working for a general contractor.

Angel Among Us

We searched for a nice apartment, and I remember years earlier my friend TJ rented a place over by the mall. We went and looked, immediately which she fell in love with the it. A very large apartment in the nicer part of town of St. Matthews, open space on the 3rd floor overlooking a large farm from the balcony window.

Surrounded by nice restaurants and local bars that should give us plenty to do with our free time together. Now from this, I started a fresh new job, new town, and new challenges. Her as well trying to manage a new place, our two dogs, trying to find work herself and we're down to one vehicle. As I sold mine so we can move into this apartment in the first place, to pay for the large down payment. Her feeling of being stuck and looking back now, I kind of see her view. Still recovering from her surgery, the pain and things started to rise with her mental stability as we both try to get accustom to a new life, in a new town.

She then came up with the idea that she wanted to be a foster parent and I thought that was a little different considering most people try to have kids of her own first. But I know how hard it was going to be, but I loved her enough to go in as a team. Well, at least I thought in my head how hard it would be. Honestly, neither one of us knew the slightest, but she said she always dreamed of helping kids. Which I'm always about helping kids when I can. I guess that's why I always had this inkling to be an elementary school teacher.

We went to thru the proper procedures, blood work, training, paperwork, everything the state of Kentucky ask for us to. And I'm proud of that, looking back now reflecting on it. It was way harder than I ever imagined it to be. With work and the things, she was dealing with internally and then trying to help kids all at the same time. With our two dogs, demands of a new job, it was all a little much, a hard challenge to say the least.

But we went to the foster home for their annual Thanksgiving dinner and then a month later for their Christmas party. The look on some of the kids faces were amazing and made you look at yourself and your upbringing a lot different. We take for granted a lot of the times, what we see as normal family life. Brothers, sisters, mom, and dad. Christmas filled with presents under the tree. It made me take a step back on how lucky I am and made me want to help more, to do more to put a smile on a kid's face.

One stuck out in our eyes, that if we ever got the chance to foster her we would. She reminded me so much of my niece, just with blonde hair, energetic, full of life and wanting to go non-stop. We asked, and the social workers said "Oh, no she's a lot of work and is already set with a foster home." My wife down, saying "she was so much fun, she's the one." And I kept saying to myself, "if it's meant to be, it will be."

And the opportunity one day came up; we would get our chance to bring her into our home and treat her as our own, and life was good. She had never been out for ice cream or frozen yogurt or even the circus. So that's what we did. We both wanted to just make her happy and enjoy our little mix family together with our two pups welcoming her in. Her playing in the floor with my two dogs licking her all over her face, surrounded by laughter.

Then like that, the foster home calls up one day and she's gone. When my wife wants to start talking about going to work again or making her own money we which this was fine with me. We didn't really have to with my job, but we just needed to watch our spending. But she wanted to make her own money, which if that's what she wanted to do. I understand that.

But things are starting to get out of control and unravel at this point. Little things are starting to get her aggravated and we would fight. We would fight about things by the end of the argument we wouldn't even know anymore what we were fighting about. But she had to win.

It is very frustrating I would do anything for this woman, just to make her happy but in the end when I learned is you must be happy with yourself before you make others happy. And maybe somewhere hidden inside us both, we weren't.

I thought at the time it was materialistic things just to please her and a just like a dreamhouse wasn't the answer for me. In the end, all you need is love. It's not seen or heard a lot of times; it's just in your soul and how it feels. But more on that later. So, from this point, we're still deep into the fostering program and trying to make someone else's world a better place.

Then we received another call from the foster home, on a rescue situation with three sisters in need of help. A twelve-year-old, a seven-year-old and eighteen months old. A rare situation, with fostering one so young. But that little girl, with strawberry blonde hair, loved me to death. The first evening when I got home from work, we had to make a run to Walmart. They came with nothing, straight from the court house. No clothes, shoes, nothing other than what they had on their backs. Truly a sad situation but we wanted to help and make them feel comfortable.

But the stresses of life came creeping in, letting little things get to us both. We tried to keep it fun and do things they all loved. Watching movies, coloring, going out for ice cream. But again, we got the call as family members began the process of taking over their care. The first was absolutely heartbreaking, the 18 months old. This little girl had to be around me 24/7. And we talked with the social workers a few times, she would cry constantly, which didn't help me and my wife's situation. And let me tell you, the lungs on this little....wooow.

But the day they called to come get her at the foster home, was when we both checked out on the idea of continuing as foster parents. This little munchkin, always in my arms and as we met the family members in the conference room to hand her over. She cried, turning towards me, reaching out with her little arms across the table. Her eyes filled with tears, crying uncontrollably reaching out for me across the table. It broke me and my wife's heart. That was the hardest thing, not the care but getting attached to these kids. Treating them like your own, and then like that, they are gone. Taken from you.

After this, both mentally and emotionally drained. We we're sitting there in our kitchen wondering what we're going to do now. She had been applying for jobs for a few weeks, and the walls of life were crashing in. Then all sudden I decided to make a change in myself and got introduced to Rhonda Byrne and the book called The Power.

This book truly changed my life, it's somewhat of a religious book; but it also talks about and quotes people from different religions and diverse backgrounds. Some of those that may not be viewed as religious at all. For the basis behind this book, it is to believe that the universe everything happens for a reason. Good, bad or indifferent when you dig deeper into it, things and events really do happen in our best interest. Even those things when faced with death, or pain, or hurt, or anger towards one another. Good can be found when we dig deeper into it; it's all a journey towards our purpose.

We all have different purposes, different dreams, different admirations, and these are the things that shape us. Whether it's God, higher power an infinite light, reincarnation or whatever source you believe in your heart. I Truly believe everything happens for reason and for the betterment of all mankind. Now from this, me and my wife are sitting one night on the couch talking about dreams. And start fantasizing about getting out of our apartment, building our own house, our own future.

I'm close to 90 days into this new outlook on life. Listening to the Power thru an audio book in the mornings to work and on the drive home. Trying to go each day with a positive outlook on life, to really take in the teachings and learnings from these philosophers. To smile and talk with strangers on the street that I meet. To learn their stories, grateful each day for the air I breathe, the family and friends I have and the life I have been given.

I took it on full force, nothing negative and as a challenge to go one full day with no negative thoughts. Then after that to shoot for a week, then a month, then three months and so on. It is a very difficult challenge, but it can make a profound impact on your life and those around you.

Not to allow negative comments, events or thoughts to enter your space. But what you find at the beginning, once you start it is more difficult than first thought.

As negative energies will hit you from all sides, all angles but once you conquer your emotional state. Your outlook on life, you tend to learn to remove them from your thinking. They are always going to be there in life, no matter what. But bounce them out of your thinking, remove yourself and thoughts out of the moment. Do so as quickly as they have entered, without affecting your state and being. I quit drinking during this time, along with a new regimen that we both had discovered to live healthier life. Try this for a day, then a week and so on, it's a great challenge to make yourself better.

After her surgery, she had been bed ridden and in pain. She began to put on some weight and was having a rough time with it. She was watching YouTube videos on ways to eat healthier and came across a

documentary called Fat, Sick and Nearly Dead that led her to find the full movie on Netflix.

If you have not seen this, or the second one on Netflix I highly recommended it. It is a practice that I have done every year since 2012 the whole month of January that I do to cleanse my body. Joe Cross documents his story of unhealthy living to living the life, that he wants. Unmedicated, healthy and free of pain.

It's a great combination of mind, body, and spirit all working together in unison towards a happy, healthy life. Do talk to a doctor or consult with a nutritionist before you start. But after watching this documentary and using some of these unhealthy eating habits myself, things made since. All the processed foods we have now in the world we live, it's in everything. Causing illness, and disease for things entering our bodies that were not intended to be consumed.

From the movie, Joe travels from Australia to America to ask people to do what they feel. That they are healthy and eat healthy. He has fresh produce and fruit with a juicing machine in the back of his car to offer a clean alternative to the daily foods we consume every day. Some ultimately refused to try this green concoction, some loved it, and others were on the fence. But if you take the time to watch, open your mind and learn what he's experienced. He was able to subdue his pain, medication, lose weight and feeling unbelievable all at the same time.

The changes that I have experienced using this, was the first 5 days my wife lost 7lbs. I myself, doing nothing other than juicing fresh vegetables and fruits was that of 15lbs in the first 5 days. Mostly around my stomach, removing the processed toxins from your body. You'll start to notice changes in your weight; your skin becomes more vibrant. Your hair but one thing you begin to notice is that your eyes become more clear. Not to mention you feel amazing, bombarding your body with super nutrients, b vitamins. Your serotonin levels start to raise, and you feel like anything is possible, a super hero, like you can run thru a brick wall.

Following this change, staying positive in life and all it brings. Really trying to evaluate myself, what I like and other's that I want to change. And taking it on full force, to be the happiest and best human being I could possibly be. Finding this new fountain of youth and happiness. Me and my wife started building momentum, setting new goals we wanted to achieve.....mostly loving life, grateful for what we have, and truly happy.

We both discussed about having a property with no neighbors, wrap around porch, log cabin quiet and tranquil for our dogs and ourselves. Envision having family and friends over for holidays thanksgiving's whatever they want to do. 3 months into listening to The Power and trying to focus on its teachings from the time I get up, till the time I go to bed, being nothing but 100% positive.

Even when negativity hits you, what the book tells you is trying to look at it at a deeper meaning. If someone is rude to you, say at a gas station or grocery store oftentimes what we don't know is what someone might be facing on the inside.

Maybe working 3 jobs to just provide for their kids at home to simple put food on the table. Being a single parent that's barely scraping by to keep them off the street. Or maybe they have a child that is terminally ill, fighting addiction or they just lost a family member unexpectedly, and they just needed to vent to someone. Just to listen, or reach out for someone to hear there story, to feel significant just for a moment.

Often, we don't really know but just take a few moments to step back, show some kind words and love. And a lot of times they reveal what's going on and who can help them. What I've also found out is that you can't get to this state with using anything that could be negative.

At this point I'm not making any more money, any more time off from work, trips or vacations, none of that. But from what I found even when I removed alcohol, listen to motivational material, juicing fruits and vegetables into my diet. The thing is my positive thinking went through the roof. My health, goals, motivation, dreams and how I felt went to a whole other level. Feeling super human almost, like I could run through a brick wall, I could do anything. With all the super nutrients entering into my body and positive outlooks on life, anything was possible. Happiness, colors, everyday things became greater.

Angel Among Us

Even when my wife wasn't fully on board reading this book and listening to it. Her negative outlook, any negative thing that came into my life didn't affect me. I started to notice that I would sing more in the mornings when I first got up, be more playful with her, be more playful with my dogs.

And the crazy thing was about 3 months in. Colors and vibrant lights throughout the day would catch my attention. And what's weird is the universe in your thinking and your positive attitude lead you to where you want to go, where your dreams are. Time seemed to slow; I became more productive, and excited about the day. Waking up everyday grateful, in absolute joy.

Now before this, I like most people love our sleep. But what changed, was through combining everything. I rarely sleep over more than 4 hrs. a day. But what's even more crazy, was that I was waking up not tired, but refreshed. Excited about the day, ready to take on my dreams and challenges of the day.

Birds I began to notice more in their flights in the sky, their singing and began to notice all these mass amounts of redbud trees began to line my 20-minute route to work. Even at the office, co-workers started to notice and take notice to my change in personality. Amazing things started happening, opportunities, everything was going in the right direction, the way I wanted life to go or at least I thought.

So, one night after one of her late-night frozen yogurt runs. We're sitting on the couch and watching some TV. I let her pick whatever she wants to watch as I played with the dogs in the floor of our apartment, just being a family. I started to think more about how we would ever get this log cabin house. How would we ever be able to afford to live on a property with no neighbors. And I kept thinking with surety, that with life. You don't need to know the exact way to achieve something, just to believe it whole heartedly that you can achieve it. Life will put you in the right situations to make them come true.

Stop saying or thinking negative thoughts. This wouldn't happen, can't happen, have the will to make it work. Whatever dreams you want and wishes; my goal is to help you achieve yours. I think in life, we all deserve and have the ability to grab our dreams. We are all unique, and our dreams are as well. Leaving room for us all to achieve them.

Deep down I don't think she ever put herself into this state, as much as I believe in this, with her and her dreams. I take it to the extreme; you have to. You have to be passionate in your dreams, to chase them and achieve them. My mom was the greatest teacher of this, how she taught us to be and how all of us kids are. We are firm believers, that if you dream it and you keep fighting towards it. You'll get it; you'll achieve it.

No, I haven't achieved all my dreams in my life, yet. And especially if I'm creating a new bucket list through this entire writing process. But the cool thing about it is that you never fail until you completely stop...

Which by that I mean you completely stop dreaming. I feel a part of you dies. To me I think you're not supposed to do that, I think that's when you begin to slowly die from the inside.

So, from this sitting on the couch and all of a sudden, my laptop goes off from a new email. Just nights prior we signed up for alerts with realtor.com, and she opens the laptop and there it sits. She's like "Clint, Clint.... Look, I think we just found it." "And I'm like what, what did you find?" And once she showed me the first picture, I was just completely blown away.

Now from this, there is no clear email address, who sent it. It just appeared with nothing else, but it's the exact house I always pictured. The one me and my mom always talked about; it's probably more than we both ever dreamed about. Now keep in mind when I and my ex-wife met. We also talked about one day owning a log cabin and wrap around porch with no neighbors. As well as I had the same discussion with my mom the night before she passed away. All three of us lined up in this life with what we wanted, other than my ex-wife wanted one particular unique feature, bamboo floors.

I thought there's no way in a million years that not only one day own an amazing piece of property like this. But to be able to find bamboo floors at the same time. It was just unthinkable, but I had a plan if I couldn't that I would install them for her. But my thoughts, thinking on life and dreams have now changed. Anything is absolutely, possible.

Well on further inspection of the property looking at pictures, gorgeous just looking like something of a state park. All these amazing redbud trees, ponds, a separate small guest house. It just seemed too good to be true, but there was one problem. There is no address and no phone number. No contact information at all. The only thing it had was they the town of Turner Station Kentucky. Now, this is the reason my wife is

thinking this is 100% a scam. "This can't be true there's no way, the price is too low, it's too perfect, etc. etc."

But with me and my new positive outlook on life, I'm learning the tools on how the universe works when it comes to dreams. That if you truly believe in yourself, your dreams and with your heart. You can manifest a dream to reality. I confirm to her "No, this is not a scam. "This is true", and I told her " I will get up early in the morning and search the ends of the Earth to find this property if I have to." It truly meant that much to me, that when I seen the pictures. I felt like my mom, her spirit was there and was going to lead me closer to her. To where I was supposed to go, to experience and the message I am to receive.

That's just how much I love her, and I wanted to make her happy, whatever it took I would do. Now my heart's racing I can't sleep at all, I'm tossing and turning all night. My dogs and her were tossing and turning as well, just a restless night. But I got up early, 4:30 in the morning, kissed my wife and my dogs. Under the cover of night, looking up at the star covered sky thinking of this amazing dream. Driving past my office in LaGrange to the Turner Station exit, thinking of this amazing property and finding this beautiful dream. One I've had ever since I was a little kid, today.... was finally going to come true. It's dark early in the morning about 5:15 and I have no direction of where I need to go other than a highway exit sign to the town of Turner Station Kentucky on the right.

So, to put backdrop on the size of this town, a very small town, homes scattered out throughout the hills, winding roads, thick forest. To think someone could just drive 40 minutes north of their apartment, early in the morning before work trying to find their dream home with no address, no phone number, no direction. Just a dream and a belief. Things that are possible, are possible.

Most would think that's absolutely insane. This world is a big place. In the chances of finding this place would be 0%. But let me tell you the events that occurred and have occurred ever since. I felt like I could not hold back anymore and not tell this amazing true story.

C. Stanton

Ch. 9. Heaven on Earth

"The greatest science in the world, in heaven and on the earth…is love"

—**Mother Teresa**

I want you to know from my heart, if we can reach such incredible heights, reach for the stars. If you can dream it up, believe it whole heartedly that you will achieve it. Never lapsing on your beliefs and dreams, willing to commit towards what you want. Your life and wishes will appear in the most amazing ways. Leading you to the story you're meant to have, the life you're meant to live. Don't let reasoning and fear keep you from your dreams. Fear is nothing more than an illusion, have faith to take on the journey and adventure…believe that anything is possible.

Fear is False Evidence Appearing Real. That's all it is. But faith by definition is a firm belief in something for which there is no proof. A firm belief is all you need to have. Things that cannot be seen but are unseen. Believe in your faith, what your heart tells you, no matter what. Face your fears and conquer them. Change your thoughts, change your life…. chase your dreams even when others tell you it's not possible.

So, begins the search for my dream home. I'm driving around on winding country roads in the early morning hours. Mix in a little fog, and the collectic Halloween scene minus the Jason or Mike Myers musical score. So about 7 in the morning rolls around going up and down winding roads, back roads passing farm after farm and I cannot find a thing. The log cabin, my dream, nothing. I drive around for hours and then I got a call from my wife, asking if I found it yet.

I unfortunately tell her "No but that I will, and I'll search again after work till I find it if I have to." This point she says again "it's a scam, quit wasting your time, etc. etc." I told her "no I believe in it and I'll find it. I'll search to the ends of the Earth to find it".

So, I call my boss at the time to let him know that I had something come up and that I won't be in till about 8:30 in the morning and then I'll work over if I must. And around this time, I'm on a back-gravel country road going up the hill and it just seems like it's going to go on forever and ever. I stopped to turn around, with huge oak trees lining the road going back down the hill. And again, as fate has it, I have two humongous bullmastiff dogs stop my wife's car in the street. Barking and climbing all over the doors and paint, I can't move. Completely disabling her car, I'm stuck on this gravel country road in BFE Kentucky.

Then out from the house walks an older gentleman in a cowboy hat, looking like he works on a farm. Flannel buttoned up shirt, dusty blue jeans and boots getting ready for his day to tend to the horses. He walks up, waves his hat around to shoooo, his dogs to get away from the car and ask, "are you lost?" "Can I help you with sumthin" in a classic southern accent. I said, "yes I'm looking for this house," and that's when I showed him a picture on my phone of the log cabin. "Do you know where it is?"

He said, "A matter of fact, I do." "I'm getting ready to head into work and it's about a mile down the road on the right on a gravel driveway and I can point you in the right direction. You can follow me down the hill." I said, "that would be excellent, thank you so much." As I follow his older turquoise Chevy truck down the road, a small gravel driveway that I passed probably 10 times searching for this property is on the right.

I didn't think of it, anything more than somebody's Farm. He kindly put on his blinker pointing to the right thru his back window. Assuring me

with a head nod that was it, he told me before to keep driving for about 5 minutes to top of the hill and there you will find the house. My mind and heart are racing as I put together that I may actually find this place.

Through these twists and turns of beautiful Kentucky countryside a small town on the edge of the Ohio River, it may actually be possible.

So, as I slowly creep up the gravel drive, I start to notice a lake off to the left and a larger cabin on the hillside. And as I'm driving slowly up, which seemed to be a 45-degree incline on this hill. I see a rundown broken barn with a single white horse off to my right.

When I make it up to the top of the hill, I start to think what if this is a wrong turn, and am I driving on somebody's farm or private property. I'm in the backwoods of Kentucky, in a spot that is definitely a No-No, but something told me to keep going on keep driving. I keep telling myself if I don't see a sign that I'll just turn around go to work and come back later tonight and search again. If I hear a single pluck from a banjo or I'm asked to squeal like a pig, anything like that…I'm so gone.

C. Stanton

But I start to notice then along this windy gravel road all these blooming redbud trees, and it triggered a memory in my mind. My grandmother has one outside of her porch in her side yard and I remember many times sitting outside drinking coffee watching my little niece playing. Talking with my mom that she mentioned that she loves that flower. When it blooms on the redbud tree at the beginning of spring, the color and that that was her favorite. Now keep in mind purple is a trigger signal for my mom and the fact that she mentioned that that was her favorite tree and seeing this flower is an instant eye opener to me.

What happened next as I started to drive more, I start to see more and more redbud trees lining both sides of that gravel driveway. So, I said, "okay that's kind of weird, but I'm just going to go with it." Crazy things have happened since she passed, pointing me in the right direction

learning to lean more on my heart to find what it seeks. Rather than relying on what my eyes and mind are telling me.

So, as I slowly drive more up on top of this hill, I look to my left and there's another lake with a crane standing on the bank, as it slowly takes off over the water. It's crystal clear and tranquil, capturing its silhouette in the clouds and the sky as it flies off, up over the top of the trees. Drawing my attention as I start driving up towards this clearing I look, and it's a panoramic view of downtown Carrollton and the valley below. It's absolutely beautiful.

Well, my mind keeps thinking what if I'm on somebody's farm, somebody's property and I'm trespassing having to be at work at this time. I'm going to get approached by police officers and possibly going to jail in this small tiny town. Or worse yet, an angry farmer shooting off his shotgun, shooting at the tires and all kinds of these things were going through my mind. I said, "Alright I'm going to keep following this crazy adventure, keep pushing forward to see if I can actually find this property." My dream house, the log cabin that I dreamed about, talking with my mother the night before she passed.

The last conversation that we ever had together, talking about dreams and ambitions, a dream home. Just about life in general after watching the movie Forrest Gump and sitting on the back porch at my grandmothers. So, I keep pushing forward, I keep telling myself I'm going to try for another minute and if there's no other signs that keep leading me the direction I need to go. I'm going to turn around, go back to work and try to find this property again later. Maybe, possibly come back up here at a different time or over the weekend to see if it is actually here.

If I keep receiving signs leading me into the direction I'm needing to go, then I'm going to continue and follow them. So, as I come around to the end of this field, I start driving into a more wooded area. Maple trees and oaks, entwined close to the road, forming a canopy kind of tunnel overhead. There branches are reaching out over the road, going towards the back part of this property. As I come around the bend, there was 25 to 30 deer grazing in the drive.

I think this is kind of weird, driving maybe 5 miles an hour and a couple of them kind of turn and look, just continue grazing. They weren't skittish or scared as I had to drive slower and weave in between a few of them and around them to get through.

Every time I've seen a deer other than the one instance when I was younger. My older brother Shane and me, we we're playing war in the backwoods by our house. This moment reminded me of the time we came upon two deer's and their two babies. I remember my older brother trying to walk up and pet one, and he got within inches of doing so. Before they turned and walked away.

Other than that time in my life, as soon as you pull up on them or get close to them, anything. They're skittish and they take off in all directions, and they're gone but not this time. They were definitely not fearful of me or anyone else up here, just peaceful and calm.

So, I'm kind of shaking my head, like what is up with this place, it's like a state park up here, it's just a different feeling. Absolutely gorgeous, peaceful, quiet. It's everything me and my mom talked about our last night with our last conversation together. And as I'm driving back, there's more redbud trees they're just everywhere, up here along the road. I drive back another minute or so and I look to my right and there's another cabin.

So, my hearts racing, I'm getting excited, closer to finding a dream. And I'm like "It's got to be here. It's got to be here, no doubt it's got to be here." To have two gorgeous cabins on the same property in the middle

of nowhere it can't be nothing more than just somebody's farm. There must be more behind the story. So, I'm like "okay, okay." "Let's just keep going, keep looking for signs, keep doing what your heart keeps telling you to do."

So, from that I drive another 30 seconds pass this property. Thinking back now there's a lot of old memories that keep coming up as I continue to write. As I come to a Tee in the road, here stands a very large Whitetail buck deer. Now I'm not a hunter, we never got into it as a kid, but I'm fine with those that do. I'm just not that type of person; I just don't think I could kill one.

But I'm thinking this is like a 12-pointer, being probably 2 feet wide maybe 230lbs, a very healthy buck. And as I'm looking our eyes kind of meet for a brief second and then he turns to start going back through the woods. Straight back the way he came and little off to the left just feet off the gravel drive... I look to my left, and I see nothing. I then look to the right and I can see a couple little cabins, almost like a resort. They're all within close proximity to each other, and they all look to be built pretty similar. In the back of my mind, I'm thinking, you can't possibly be to the right.

Because it supposed to have 40 acres all its own and from the picture I seen, I could see no other properties, no other houses, no neighbors, no nothing. So, from this, I make the decision to go left. And as I'm left, I look to the right again, and I see that same deer calmly walking thru the woods probably 20 feet from the road. So, I come around to the left, then a swooping right, as I comes down thru a little dip in the road and then comes back up again.

There's a little left, and it starts to continue up towards a clearing to the right. As I'm driving along here comes two more deer across the road, out of the field calmly crossing the front of my wife's car. Whitetails

pointing upward, then disappearing in the green clover over the hillside to the left. At this point I'm driving really slow now, just taking it all in. All the beauty of nature, the fields, the trees. The redbud trees that keep lying along the gravel drive. Then as I get closer my eyes are drawn to the right, I see a Buddha statue sitting on some rocks under a Japanese red Maple over looking the hillside.

I'm thinking this is kind of weird and random to have that out in the middle of nowhere Kentucky, and I'm still not seeing this house. "Where are you hiding?" But something keeps telling me to continue, something is truly special about this place and I follow the drive as it sweeps to the left once again. And as I'm coming up to slight hill from that field with the Buddha statue, I look to my left and I see a little pond. It seemed familiar, closely to the one pictured in the original email sent to us the night before. I look to my right and I see the clearing for the guest house that was pictured as well in the original email so now my heart's pumping, it's pumping, it's pumping.

I continue going, up the drive to the last little hill and I look to the right. Just thru a small clearing of bare trees, I was able to see the brown-red cedar wood on the face of the house. Still not believing what's transpired, how I was brought to this point to find this place but it's just surreal, a miracle. How all these signs leading my heart and me to this place. I tear up, thinking the odds and possibility of being brought to this point is unbelievable.

Searching my whole life to find it. Doubting all these years, till I changed my mind, my beliefs on what is possible. We can truly create miracles in our life, and others. It's more beautiful than I could have ever imagined in my dreams or could have imagined talking to my mom the night before she passed. But here it was, as I'm pulling in. Coming past the last clearing of the trees. A slight wind blowing through the branches as I come to the top of the drive to make the final right at the top of the property and just stop.

I stopped just outside the front gate, to get out and take a deep breath. Closing my eyes, to take in the soft, warm breeze and morning air on my skin. Arms stretched out wide, as I slowly open them, reaching out to the heaven's above. To say, "Thank you." "Thank you for this moment, this unbelievable journey."

I felt like the trees, the flowers, the breeze all here is all my mom. I felt like she led me here, to fine this amazing place and to share this unbelievable true story. To have the faith to believe in the unseen, to have the faith that she's still around guiding all of her kids. Like a warm hug, she put her arms around me and smiled down from Heaven. As I call my wife with exciting to tell her "no I found it."

Ch. 10. Finding a Dream

"My dream home exists just for me. It's waiting for me to find it. I believe this with all my heart."

—Anonymous

"No, I found it!" And with calling her it was very exciting, and I could feel she was excited over the phone looking back now it's hard to believe. I think in a few days she would understand why it was so amazing. To find this place with all the twists and turns, windy country roads and hills. In the beauty from this amazing place. Being locked away in a little part of Kentucky, it's just special to me and always will be. From there I went up to the front door, knocking a couple of times with no one answered.

I searched inside my wife's car and found some scrap paper to leave a note. I left my name contact information, my cell phone number on the front door of the house. And then also got some scrap paper and left another note on the windshield of a Dodge Ram that was pictured in the email photo of the house as well. From here I'm taking pictures, send them to her, which she's super excited, still she can't believe I found it. As I'm calling to talk on the phone, our minds were racing and super excited about creating this dream. That only a few months ago, it was just that, a dream. As I'm coming back out to the driveway, back on to the open clearing never in a million years would I have ever pictured this.

An older Vietnamese man running a backhoe over top of the panoramic clearing, with an Amish guy working hand in hand. Setting large flat slate river rocks in the field forming a beautiful walkway up to a panoramic overlook on the hillside.

So, I stop the car to walk over to them and they seem to be shocked dressed in a nice suit fighting the wheat and brush to get to them. Now I ask who owns the property in the back. I was sent an email late last night about it, and I'm highly interested in purchasing it. But it didn't have any contact information, no phone number, agent number nothing all. It was just a picture and a town listed in the description, and that was it. So now the Vietnamese guy is very confused as he knows how hard and secluded this place is to find.

And that's where I told him "I had things and events that just led me here once I got off the exit and that's how I'm standing in front of you right now." Still shocked and bewildered he acknowledge the strategy of it. He proceeds to tell me that he doesn't own the property, but he does have some of the property up there on the hillside. But he does know the people that own it.

He told me to turn back around and go to the T in the road. From there you'll go to the right and then make a left towards the other cabins nestled along the wood line on the property. They will be the last house on the right and they are home actually right now.

So, I did, and I turn back around to do just that, to introduce myself and ask about the property. I'm super excited now right now and that I'm actually going to talk to these people get their contact information and start working out negotiations on purchasing this property.

Angel Among Us

One that is beyond what I and my mom talked about or ever envisioned, beyond my wildest dreams. So, as I pull up, I park up on the hillside and walk down to the front door. A Beautiful cabin that has a pond in the front, some nice trees not to mention more of the redbuds all over the property.

My heart's pumping and I go to knock on the door ring the doorbell. Shortly after the doorbell rings, an elderly Vietnamese woman and her sister come to answer the door. I introduce myself and said, "My name

is Clint and I had an email on this property late last night and have been searching since 4 o'clock this morning to find it." "The one over the hillside, with the 40 acres on the backside of this property." They were all kind of shocked as to how I was able to find it. That's why I was searching so long and that I was the first person to ask about it. I then begin to inform them the reason as to why I believe that I the first person to ask about it. It's because in the email that I was sent. There was no address or phone number just the listing price, the pictures. No agent information and just the town that it was in, nothing else.

They asked if I want to come in and talk for a little bit and I said "Absolutely!" And I started telling the story that I've been dreaming of a house like this, my whole life and that my mother had a dream of once living in a log cabin with no neighbors. A wrap around porch spending Christmas' and thanksgivings out in the Country in a cabin.

And from this, they're excited and I continue telling them, that this is the last conversation we had before she passed away the next morning. And I would do whatever it takes to find it one day. "I would like to purchase property for your asking price." Now they're super excited and what they tell me next is weird.

They begin to mention that they both had a dream that someone in a suit would come this morning, knock on the door and asked about the house. They had no idea how they got there; something kept leading them here to this place, this morning. From this, they ask "Would you like to come in, have something to drink and talk?" I said, "Unfortunately I do not have much time as I'm already late for work, but it was worth it finding this place and finding them." But I told them all that I would be back tomorrow if it was alright to show my wife and my dad the property. So, I thanked them and went on my way to work.

Heart pumping and full of excitement. I briskly drive to work. The grin on my face ear to ear, even though I'm 45min late. At that moment it didn't matter. What mattered was finding a dream, having the courage to follow my heart, right where I was supposed to be. Headed to work and super excited to get home, sending pictures as I leave to my wife. Super excited to go out and celebrate the next night once I get out of work. I then talked to my dad and then to her mom. To set up for a meeting after work to show them the property. So, I am waiting patiently all day excited for work to be over with.

Then the rush home to take a quick shower, grab my ex-wife our two dogs and start to head north on Interstate 71. My dogs being that are super excited because they loved going on car rides. I have the mini pin name Roo and her dog named Charlie ready to set sail on this new adventure.

We get them a throw blanket laid out to put them on our laps for the drive from St. Matthews. Calling her mom on the way, they're excited as she is already heading south on 71. With my dad probably 5 minutes behind her.

Setting everything up and where to meet us off the exit at Turner Station. It is from there, finally having everyone meet up. I told my dad that I have to drive him up the hill, that he will not be able to find this place.

Describing what it looks like thru pictures and everyone was super excited including my two pups. I told him "It would take about 5 to 7 minutes to get up there on the hill, so I'll make sure to drive extra slow because of all the winding roads and turns we have to take." A Sunny 5 o'clock afternoon in a late April on a Tuesday in Kentucky. And the crazy thing I noticed with the drive, all along the highway, was nothing but blooming red bud trees all along the trip. Once off the exit, her mother was waiting off the side of the road. My dad, I called and was 5min behind her.

Once off the exit, we were lined up in the grass with our blinkers on. My dad pulled in behind, and I got out with excitement and walked up to his driver side window. Dad, I said just follow us up the road it's a little windy, but we should be up on top of the hill and at the property in 5 to 10 minutes. A cigarette in between his teeth, grinned and said "Okay." Driving through the small town of Turner Station. Passing over some train tracks, working away through the hills of Kentucky.

So, once we got close to an old farm barn on the right. I told him there will be a gravel driveway to the left and you start working our way up the hill to the property. So, once we reach this point and start making a left to go up the gravel drive. I'll drive slow enough to where they can take it all the scenery and slowly pull into the property. Around the corner at the top of the hill there's a gate that opens up and leads down to the log cabin and then the drive going around a circle tree.

So, we come in, then pull up to the right and get out. Once we get out, her mom's face showed all. How super excited she was, my dad's looking around smiling and I know he's thinking this is crazy. I had both say, "How in the world did you ever find this place?" And I told my dad, "I felt like my mom was leading me here." All the things that brought me here, the redbud trees all along this driveway, all around up here, it's just heaven on earth.

They all get out and walk around letting the dogs run carefree like crazy people. Smiling, tails wagging and my ex-wife, ex-mother-in-law walking around in awe of this place. Minds were racing, thinking about ideas to create on this beautiful piece of property.

Let me tell you about the sunsets up here. All of the colors, peach, orange and the blues mixed with purples in the sky. It's always been a favorite of mine, but up here it's more vibrant. Like an amazing color painting, just painted for you. That color combination of blues and peach in the sky, mixed in with purples. When you see it, you sit back and just take notice, you take in all its beauty.

Fast forward to 3 days later me and my ex-wife are super excited going to one of her local places to have dinner. Happy hour for drinks, tasty steak at a local Logan's restaurant in St Matthews. We started having a couple of drinks, sitting at the bar, as her bartender friend poured the rounds. She was wondering why I and my ex-wife were so ecstatic and happy.

I started telling her this crazy story about finding our dream house. A log cabin wrap around porch, no neighbors and having bamboo floors. She looked at us, the same as I did. Bewildered at this as to how am I ever going to find a log cabin with bamboo floors.

That was what my wife wanted, but I never thought in a million years I would find one with it. And then I would just add bamboo floors later down the road for her. But we did, and it was a gift. We proceeded to tell her this amazing story all these crazy events that happened to find this property 40 minutes north of here. With all the twists and turns, country roads, I should have never been able to find it. But with my mom in the background, somehow, she let me do it, and I truly felt this. And this is when the story gets really crazy.

So, after me being super excited and telling her some parts and pieces of the story. I had an older couple come up to me, probably in their mid-sixties and ask him to tell the story. They invited me and my ex-wife over to the table and said "Would you guys mind telling that story to my wife?"

And when I started to tell the story about getting a random email, things of that nature. I'm sitting on the outside of the table. His wife is diagonal from me on the inside of the booth directly across from my wife. She stops and puts her hand out in front of her face and says, "You look like your mom, don't you?" Now keep in mind I've never met these people, nor have I ever seen them before and they just want to hear this amazing story.

So, I'm kind of shocked, and I haven't even mentioned the fact that my mom has passed on. I look to my right at my ex-wife, and she's in shock as well. Then the lady continues. "You have the same bone structure in your cheeks and face not to mention you have the same blue eyes." Now I'm just in total shock and disbelief at this point. I'm not sure quite sure what to say next. Her husband asked me to continue on what the story. And I think his wife put together that my mom has passed on at this point. She's visibly upset and ask to leave the table, and I ask" is everything okay?"

Her husband proceeds to let her out from the booth, then touches her on the arm and says, "honey I'll be right there." Turns with his head over his shoulder, sticking his hand out saying, "I'll be right back, don't leave." But says "we've been looking for a log cabin like this to retire in and can you call these people to set up a meeting with them about the other property?" I said, "Yes absolutely, I'll call them right now," so I go outside to the front parking lot to make the phone call.

I call Ann, along with her sister and the teacher. The teacher is a Buddhist monk that helped create this beautiful place, which explains some of its astonishing landscapes. To let them know that I found a potential buyer that was interested in their log cabin, that they were wanting to sell. This was great news as they were ready to move to Arkansas to build a new retreat and sanctuary. So about 2 to 3 minutes in, they became very excited. Thanking me for helping them find people interested in the property.

At this point, the older gentleman approaches me at the front of Logan's asking me to get off the phone!!! I was a little confused and he was adamant about me getting off the phone at this point. His wife was visibly upset, had left and I wasn't sure what was going on. At this point, I tell Anne, everyone that I must get off the phone, but I'll call her back. So, I'm really confused and I'm thinking this guy is really upset and is wanting to fight me or something. I wasn't quite sure what was going on.

So, I do and he's like "I don't want you to get upset or think anything other than what I'm about to tell you." He continues and says, "my wife is not a medium, she's not a psychic but when you came to our table and was starting to tell the story about how you came about finding this property." "And the dream you've always had of having a log cabin with a wrap-around porch." My wife said that a lady appeared on your left shoulder with blackish-gray salt pepper hair, short haircut around 5 foot 7 to 5-foot 8 medium build.

She had your same eye color and leaned down to you while looking at my wife and uttered these words. "Baby boy, I love you, I miss you, and I'm happy I was able to help you find this place." Now that was my mom, short and to the point but what's crazy is the baby boy phrase.

I still have a guitar radio that I won for singing the week before I left for Nashville and it's still one of my most treasured possessions. It has notes from all my family and friends before I left for Nashville to pursue my dream as a singer-songwriter.

What the note on the side base of the guitar that is it from my mom. And one of the first thing she says in the note is. "Baby boy always remember to keep God in your soul and a song in your heart and always be a dreamer. Love Mom." "Be a dreamer and chase those dreams baby boy," she would say.

So that hit a chord with me, and she use to say this to me as well. Then he proceeds to say that "There was another older lady with her, with white blondish hair." I am a complete wreck at this point in tears. I'm fearful as I'm thinking it's my grandmother Shelby, my mom Sandra's mom.

She has been sick with pneumonia, and I'm thinking she may have passed on now. She's with my mom up in heaven, then appearing in here together to somebody I don't even know at a Logan's restaurant in Louisville Kentucky. Wiping my tears away, he sees that I'm upset. Bawling my eyes out in the waiting area, but I had to call my grandmother and to make sure she was okay.

I call my grandma, and on second or third ring with my heart beating she picks up, and she can tell I'm upset. She asked how I am and if everything is okay and I said "Yes, Grandma I was just calling to make sure you're okay." "I just had a crazy amazing thing that just happened to me and involves mom and it's hard to explain but I'm glad you're okay." "I'll call you back here shortly, but I have something else I have to take care of first." At this point, my ex joins me in the waiting room and asks if I'm okay and I said "yes." I go back to meet back up with them to the table to finish telling the story.

Now, this point her husband knows that his wife has just described my mom that passed on, years prior and somebody else is with her, and we've never met. But he felt like he had been here before and this moment. And wanted to make sure that he could come up to see the property because that was a dream him and his wife have...

What I didn't know that before we sat down at this table to have this conversation. He was meeting his wife of 23 years to talk about getting divorced. And after this story, in this meeting by chance, they decided to give it another try. That things happen for a reason, but I don't believe in things by chance. I think it's all designed to lead us where we're supposed to go, who were supposed to meet, if we look for the signs.

After finishing the story, describing how I found it, how I felt and all the beauty of this place. He's beyond excited now, wanting to go up and set up a meeting to view this other cabin. But we can't do it till the weekend, the earliest which is Saturday morning be the earliest.

We end up pushing it back to 4 on Saturday because his son had a baseball game to go to. I told him "That's fine, and I would meet him off the exit to show him the way up to the property and introduce them to the owners of the other cabin." We decided to head up earlier to take some pictures and walk around the property some more. And once he called, we would come down the hill to meet them on the side off the road. As does my little niece Ashlee, my brother Shane's son Tyler along with my mother in law and boyfriend Joe join us as well.

We all meet off the side of the road, off the exit again. The older man from Logan's decides to bring his teenage son along for the trip. I kindly get out to introduce him to my dad, my mother-in-law and the whole crew. I tell them as I told my family a few days early that it will take about 5 to 7 minutes to get up to the property. Super excited I could see it in his boy's eyes, and we hopped in our vehicles to begin turning up the hill.

We get back to the to the Tee to make a right to go to the back cabin and once I get out. The guy mentions that he feels like he's been here before. I said, "I know the first time I came up here I felt that way it's just a different place." "It's like having your own personal state park up here." When he gets out the car, he stops and says, "that's weird."

And I said, "What's weird?" He says, "The address 1492, I use for all my toolbox combinations at work, working out at the Ford plant." I think that's weird connection because my grandfather, my mom's dad Curt worked and retired from Ford back home in Cincinnati. As I'm walking up to this beautiful place and going to knock on the door and introduce everyone to Anne and the teacher.

So, from this point, we all gather it into the living room and I start introducing everyone. Then the teacher, Anne and her sister, I start having them tell their side of the story. How they all had a dream about someone just showing up in a suit, knocking on the door, asking to buy the property.

And from this, everyone walks outside to relax and check out the back of the property. Then I start telling my side of its things, what led me to here, all the different scenarios and little signs leading me to this wonderful place. Then my dad notices magnolia trees all around this cabin, all around this property. And I mentioned him earlier about all the redbud trees lining the mile and half driveway. The thing is, that mom always love that flower and that tree is her favorite. She loves when they bloom and gave off that purple color.

When I start telling my side of the story, my dad mentions to me that there's all these magnolia trees heading up the drive. That his mother loves those especially when they bloom. "Have you ever seen them, they're kind of ugly until they bloom this huge beautiful flower?" So, as I start telling my side of the story and leading up to me revealing to him what happened in Logan's just a few days ago. I turn to my dad to watch his reaction. As well as my niece, my mother-in-law, as I asked Ashley my ex-wife to keep it from everybody and to let him reveal it. A perfect stranger, who didn't know me. None of my family, my background and in a perfect moment a chance meeting, we were giving a beautiful gift.

So, as he goes on to tell his side of the story and describes what his wife revealed to him. Describing my mom to a T. The emotions and tears start to fill his eyes, and as he continues, I don't know of the second person yet who is with my mom.

"Yes, there was a second lady with white blondish hair and a bob haircut." At this point me and my dad look at each other, tears in our eyes. As everyone else, there is uncertain why? My niece comes over to give me hug on the back deck and ask if I'm ok. Well, the only person in our family, that matches that description, was the one my dad was talking about with the magnolia trees. His mom, my other grandmother who had passed away 3years prior to my mom's passing. But they somehow were there together, in that moment appearing to strangers, to deliver a message.

So, after this revelation, I'm in sheer utter shock. My thoughts on life, the things around us, about my mom, feelings in general. Early signs several years, it's all starting to come together. No, we're not alone, there is something past this life. The ones we love, those who have come and gone are still around us. We just can't see them, but through love, we can feel their soul and spirit. If there was anyone that is able to do it, it was my mom.

She loves her kids, being a mother and everything that comes with. The good and the bad, whatever it takes to give to her kids, it was done. She loved our friends and treated each one like her own, like family. Never to have met a stranger, just like her father. A heart that can sense others in pain, if you were talking BS, she would call you out on it. But in a loving way, to help you learn and grow to becoming a better, well-rounded person. Short with her words, but to the point with love.

So, I arrange a meeting for all my closest friends and family. Anyone my mom ever cared about or loved. I showed them pictures tell them that I would like for all of them to come to the property. I had to take a big convoy up the hill and I like to be a part of this and a part of the story they let me do it. So, at this point putting everything I had down on this place, eating out of my apt getting into this new house. Some say money was tight, it was pretty tight and I made pretty good money at my current job. But I had my brother's stepson Tyler with me who's was going with me to get some food, but I didn't know what to get and wasn't quite sure how it's going to afford to pay for food for everybody up on the on the hill. But I kept the faith, as long as you stay positive about it, things typically seem to work out the way they should.

I'm leaving to go get food, and I noticed that it's raining and there's an older woman walking in the rain with her grandson. I stopped to turn around and pulled over to ask if they need a ride to where they're going? "That would be wonderful." "You know we're just going to this church up the street, and we're stuck in the rain."

So, I start talking, ask them where they're from just chit-chat. They asked us what we were doing today, and I told him that we were going to go pick up food for a party. I'm bringing together all my family and friends to tell them this amazing story about my mom who led me to this property. She said "You can drop us off at the front doors. My grandson has autism, but he seems to be around calm around you." "Just come in really quick and tell our pastor your story." "They love hearing things like this." Me with excitement I do, telling them an abbreviated version of this story.

Then they brought out all this chicken, all this mashed potatoes and gravy, mac and cheese and sweet tea. Please have it; we'll have to throw it out. We had a church function earlier and we gave away all we could, and you still have plenty more. If you take it and use it for your family and friends for the party.

So, after some convincing I did. Tyler looked at me in amazement, like I just happened to be picking up some random people and then they give us enough food for all of us up there later day. I said "I don't know, it's just weird how things work out when you least expect it." We go and pick up my ex-wife and start heading north on 71 to meet family and friends. Leading them all up to the property and to tell him this crazy, amazing story.

Having 30-40 of my closest family and friends waiting for us off the exit. I told my father days earlier not to mention the story and how it was revealed to anyone yet. How my mom and his mom were together in a Logan's restaurant. Reaching out to deliver a message to us, our family. To total strangers and to let us all know that they are ok.

Now telling the story to my family and friends it just came naturally. Such a nice summer day, in the middle of May and bringing them all up there together to tell them this unreal story.

That their mom was still around still watching over us. Remembering the look on their faces and especially best friend Brian, shedding some tears. As well as my friends Corey and Mandy. I and Corey met for a past job at a local computer business. They were there for me after losing my mom, as we had many discussions about parents being gone.

Now telling this part of the story and them being there I hope it meant something for him as well. Him losing both of his in high school, knowing what we were going thru as a family and knowing how rough things can be. But to tell it and then to have my friend Brian come up and give me a big hug as my mom loved him like a son. But moving him enough, in such a way that he's not normally accustomed. Changing if not just for that day, what this life is about. Having felt like he's had bad luck all his life, and all the hardships. But this story reached him and made him think of what was possible.

Ch. 11. Or so I thought

"Put your back against the wall against adversity. As the only way to move, is forward thru them."

—Eric Thomas

As I Tell them the real story seeing the tears flow from friends and family. I realize some things we don't understand, some things we often feel and don't see can happen. I'm not quite sure when it started to fall apart, when my ex started to act out and reveal her true self. Not quite sure if it was me, the property, being alone away from everything or maybe changes in my work schedule and demands I'm still to this day not quite sure, but I'm ok with that. I gave more than any one person probably ever would for love.

I can hold my head high in knowing that, and I hope ultimately, in the end, she and I are better from it. That I would have done anything for love, for her and that it's ok. Its ok that we fell apart and went our separate ways. Life and its journeys take us where we need to go. Life sometimes brings others together, and then sets us on different paths. And I just want you to know, that I forgive. 😊

We have since had this talk, and even during the final days, she could not quite understand it, but I learned to first forgive myself. I was by no means perfect, but then ultimately, I needed to forgive her. To hopefully heal and move on from this madness.

It started to unravel 2 months after this perfect journey finding our dream house. Having big dreams of a family and a home everything we both ever wanted. She started saying that she was stressed out and I was kind of confused by this. And she was the one that was wanting to move to a new city, a new town, a new adventure. I was making great money at the time, so she didn't have to work.

But she started wanting to take trips with her cousin, then meeting new friends. And at first, I was ok with it, I trusted her and if she felt like she needed a little time away it didn't bother me, I just wanted her to be happy. That's all I ever cared about was her happiness, and my dreams became hers. We were one with one another. But looking back, there were signs, and I guess it is what they say, love is blind.

Being married is a totally different ball game. I always had in my mind how it would be, how I didn't want to be in an unhappy, unhealthy relationship, an unhealthy married couple. I wanted to grow old together, have adventures and all our dreams to come true.

But sometimes you lose, sometimes that person you think you know doesn't even truly know themselves. And this is one of those unfortunate cases, maybe deep down I tried too hard. I just tried to love her the best way I knew how and gave my all to this person. To help her with all our dreams, it was never going to be enough. Because deep down inside she was living a lie, a lie to me and herself. I'm not sure if through all of this, the fact that she felt alone out there or just her conscience on who she was and what she truly wanted. But it definitely opened a door; I felt betrayed and hurt. Broken hearted.

Now, this all started to unravel about 2 to 3 months into being out there. She wanted to take trips alone, going with her cousin, with friends I'm not allowed to meet. Huge red flag people, which if it wasn't for the commitment of marriage I would have ran. If you find yourself in a similar situation. "Run for your life people !!!!" LMAO!

But I was in it till the end (a song dedicated to my wife "Love me till the End") I always dreamed of meeting that one person. That one who knocks you off of your feet and you can't see yourself ever without them. But once up there, she never wanted to spend time with me out there or our dogs. Saying that she was always stressed and needed time away. I wanted to give her everything she ever wanted, I guess that's the part where love is blind.

But through all this, even the worst of times there are steps you can take to get through it. You can make a change, that you can learn to love yourself more, and even though your love for someone else may become lost. There comes a point where you cannot let them walk all over you. You can't make them change you into something that you don't want to be. You have to learn to make a stand, what you feel is right in your heart and your soul.

The first thing she did is she starting not coming home, like at all. And I started having feelings of her cheating. And trust me this is one of the toughest things I ever went through in my life. But looking back I'm starting to understand her and her mental state. You start to understand the inner torments that she must have had at that time.

She would be gone weeks on end acting out on me, screaming at the top of her lungs. Just trying to fight with me on all fronts. If she said, the sky is green, knowing that it's blue. She would argue that it was green till the end of time.

I'm not sure why she changed her love for me and how it went away. I'll probably never know. But what I did know is that I was put here for a reason, taking this job put in a situation around some amazing people. One of the steps I took after that night finding out, most importantly was to learn how to love myself. I started to release the control she had over me, my decisions and my life. I really started to focus on myself and what I wanted.

I started a bucket list filled with exciting adventures and things I wanted to experience. Some that looking at it will be hard, if not impossible to achieve, but how the universe works. Our creator finds mysterious ways to make them happen. I continued to listen to motivational speakers and speeches.

Jim Rohn, Tony Robbins, Eric Thomas, Les Brown, Jack Canfield to name a few. I try to listen to them first thing in the morning at least for 10minutes to start my day off on the right foot. Creating a bucket list and writing things down that I always wanted to do or accomplish became fun. Goal setting to move in the direction of your wishes. If you don't know where you want to go, how can you possibly know the path that you need to take to get there...

And the thoughts of positive thinking and the teachings of Dr. Masaru Emoto. The power of the most precious resource on our planet, water. And our need throughout the universe to sustain life. Our bodies are made up of

60% water, but our hearts and brain are composed of 73%.

His work and findings of the human consciousness has a direct effect on the molecular structure of water. That water could react to both positive and negative thoughts. What does that teach us about our own thoughts, bodies and soul? We are what we think, and the universe can manifest your thoughts. "It is the blueprint for our reality." "Emotional energies can change the physical structure of water." If the world we know are mostly water, what does that teach us of how thoughts, can shape and mold our reality.

And then there was a time finding out that the love of your life is not who you pictured it to be. And no matter how much you love something, it's a give and take. It's kind of hard to say which is the worse pain to overcome. That of losing my mom without a warning or going through a divorce with somebody that you thought loved you but in their own mind, they don't love themselves. In life people in this state, they tend to hurt those they love the most, who would do anything for them.

I had to learn that the hard way and I'm not proud of it, but I'm glad I made the decision I did. So, I can help other people that may feel they don't deserve to be in this life. That they have the family that they do. That they have the amazing friends, that they have the love, that they have people in their life every day, that they deserve. That we are stronger than we think and can change the world.

There is a certain amount of people that I would like to thank that saved my life. One being God, the higher power, Infinite light, whatever it maybe or whatever you believe. I don't judge others thinking of what this life's all about, their beliefs and dreams of what this world can be.

Another is being put in the position in LaGrange Kentucky. A little small town just outside of Louisville, I truly do think everything happens for reason.

And I think I was put in that position to meet two close friends, to help me thru. Placed in my life at just the right moment, to save mine. Mr. Bill White and Miss Marsha Moore. You really don't know exactly what you meant to me or did for me at this time. But you both just taking time, to ask me how my day was. Taking 5 precious minutes out of your day to say "Hello, how is your day." "Is everything okay." "Is everything alright?" "Do you need anything?" This meant the world to me, that others do care, and it changed me for who I am. When I see somebody that's obviously feeling hurt or sensing pain or just having a bad day.

Taking five minutes, this could mean the world to them; it could save somebody's life. We never know what someone else is going through or facing in this present moment.

For my nephew's Andrew, Carter and Hunter, my niece Ashlee. One day I hope you all know what you mean to me and the pictures of them I carry in my wallet that saved my life. Knowing how much they love me, their uncle. Knowing how much those kids love me, enjoying me being around, making them happy I couldn't hurt them. I couldn't do it no matter how much she was hurting me and then my family. I couldn't do it.

And then looking inside my dream house, log Cabin with wrap around porch. Everything I've ever wanted and then going upstairs to the loft. Things I have built for my wife, closets, a log bed. Things that she wanted, that mattered to her. Then seeing a white sheet on our bed and thinking this is it. I don't deserve to be here anymore, it's still to this day hurts and brings me to tears.

No matter what happens be in a grateful state, a beautiful state. Depression's focus is on you, not others. It is selfish, don't let it be, don't face it alone. Reach out to loved ones, those around you. Change your state of thinking. Find beauty in whatever life brings you, whatever moves you. It's a short trip.

I'm not ashamed of this, and furthermore, I embrace it. Knowing that it pushed me to be a better person, these moments pushed me to be the man I am today, the man I'm striving for. Finally knowing my purpose, finally knowing that I'm here to touch people with my music, in my words and poetry, that's my gift. Knowing how to see someone, I guess you can call it being a noticer. And knowing how they feel, locked deep inside. If they're in need or just need to talk. That's my gift, that's what I'm able to find, that's what I'm able to do. To touch others through words and from the heart.

Because you never know what that person is going through, or why they may be rude or upset or act the way they do. You may not know they are fighting cancer or just lost a family member, a job or a beloved pet. Maybe finances are the issue; you just don't know what's going on till you ask. Why I always try to treat people with respect and love. I try to understand what may be driving them to act the way that they do.

Knowing I'm doing finally what I was supposed to do, to help people to answer why they maybe feel this way or are going through this pain. How to access the events that happen in our lives, some wanted, some unwanted. Form a plan on how to address it. What you're able to do from this event, then ultimately learn and grown from it.

But I think the one thing that stopped me was, I just remember my three dogs. I had four at one point but sadly had to give one away. His name is Bear. I had a friend from work take him in, and he spends his days outside playing with his daughter. Or sitting out by the bank fishing with him at the lake behind their house. But I still think of him every now and then. For all of my pups, I'm so thankful to have them in my life because of her.

Giving me Charlie, my dotson beagle black and tan who has epilepsy but that dog loves life more than anything, always smiling. More than any dog I've ever seen in my life, and he gave it back to me. I think dogs they can sense things and he was the one I remember sitting in front of me overlooking the Loft. In front of the banister crying, me looking over the railing, then to him. Over the railing, and back at him with his eyes piercing into my soul. I just fell to the floor, and he just sat there, putting his little puppy dog paw on my knee. And I couldn't do anything but look at him.

He began to lick my face and from there I wipe my eyes, threw the white sheet down from the bed over the side. Giving his sad puppy dog look he had on his face and I just felt like he was saying. "Dad don't do nothing stupid, don't do this, it'll be okay, it'll be fine." It seemed like tears were welling up in his eyes. And I just drop that blanket, hugged him and then I remember the other dogs coming up, climbing up the steps, all around me, wagging their tails uncontrollably. My heart was just filled with love.

From that moment, when I grab my dog Charlie I gave him a hug went to my knees on the ground he put his little paws around me and then moose and bear and Roo, my little miniature kangaroo Pinscher. All rescues, I got them all from the pound, the best dogs I could ever ask for. As they all come up the steps, running, wagging their tails and licking on me and just showing me love. That's exactly what I needed in that moment.

And from that point, I went down to the kitchen, continued to cry some more, vulnerable I was surrounded by my pups and their love. They are my kids, my fur babies; I enjoy spoiling them in every moment that I get and enjoy cuddling with them nightly.

I felt at that time; I couldn't talk to my family it was so embarrassing. I felt every time when they brought her up it was something negative and I couldn't control what she was doing. I couldn't do anything to change the situation. It was slowly driving me insane, driving me to be a person that I didn't want to be.

A negative person that doesn't notice a beautiful sunrise in the morning, to the sun sets at night and the stars in the sky. Family, friends and little things that they do in your life, I just wasn't grateful. That I let one person and their actions take away who I was. Taking away the special parts of my being, my heart, and my soul. I had to learn the old saying; if you truly love somebody, you must learn to let them go. Because they say if you learn to let go and they come back, it was meant to be.

As I continued down downstairs to the kitchen and decided that I wasn't going to let her win. I wasn't going to give in, give somebody all of me when they didn't deserve me. I grabbed a picture out of my wallet that had my little nephews and my niece, then a picture of my mom and saying I wrote on the back.

Matthew 7:7 "ask and it will be given to you; seek and you shall find; knock and the door will be opened to you." From there I searched through the Bible, just words from

God, the higher power seeking for answers as to why I was put on this Earth. Why I'm here, why I'm going through this, seeking to really get those answers. What I did get was a journey, a stepping stone towards these answers period. Towards that purpose why we are all here.

How to grow positivity in your life. The events of our lives, do not have to shape us, control them. Encourage each other, build it. Build a world full of love. There is already enough hate. Learn not to be quick to react, being resentful and bitter. Take on the challenges; life gives you. Grow and defeat them. Act on them. Be prepared for the challenges.

Studies have been done where people have had near death experiences. Of different religions and background and as they recall seeing a bright light. Seeing God, and sometimes only hearing a voice asking two questions. "How did you expand your ability to love?" and "What wisdom did you learn?" How many of us, seeing these questions could answer them honestly, clearly? How many of us would look at these two questions and feel unfulfilled. That if we could ask these questions on our life, how would we change, learn from it and grow.

And you should ask questions. And if you look hard enough, you will get those answers you seek. And if you believe, it may not always be the answer that you're searching for. But it's the answer that you need. We look years down the road and recollect troubled times that are a part of life, good times that are a part of life, and you seem to find out that those trials and tribulations. Things that you went through are exactly what you needed to shape you and what you believe. Even with losing my mom. It was one of the hardest things I've ever experienced. I hope none of you ever experience the shocking loss of a parent or loved one with no warning.

But what I did focus on was that of my sister, coming up the street in pain and just screaming. It wasn't registering then that it was my mom period. But what I focused on was being strong for her, helping ease her pain anyway I could. Then once she uttered those words for the third time laying in the street. My mom, with all the good did she did that week, all things that she talked about for years that she completed.

Then if they would have went on their vacation my mom and dad's anniversary with my sisters for one final trip together. If she would have passed away along the trip or down there in Myrtle Beach. How much harder it would have been on all of us not knowing what happened. Not having her in her own bed, at peace. Having to figure things out on how to get her back to northern Kentucky to be buried.

When you look deep down, you can find even in the worst hurt, grace.

And I was thinking at this moment being alone in the cabin, the dream me, and my mom always had. I was grateful that my dogs were with me, in the fact that they were able to show me love and gratitude for what I did have. A loving family, loving friends and those crazy pups. That is the greater scheme of things, this house and all its beauty mean nothing, all you truly need is love.

That's all you really need. The dream I always had as a kid and shared with my mom.... was just that. It was only a house, and with out love, never became a home. Without love, this dream would never manifest itself. It would never become reality. It would never become what I first thought, heaven on earth.

Having not from my mom, striving us to be better, to be the kids she always saw us to be. Chasing hopes and dreams. Pushing us all towards our own individual goals. Never judging and always striving forward, the right way, with no judgement...only that of love.

Laying there with my phone on google to the new testament. Reading passages that related to my relationship with my ex-wife or lack thereof...I believe thru it all, I was at the right place, at the right time. Surrounded by the right group of people in my life.

I sent out a text to our company chaplain, which this job was the first that I ever had one, let alone this type of support in the work place. I just sent him a brief text, asking to talk first thing in the morning and if he could come see me at my office first thing when he got in. "Sure; and is everything alright." I was brief, taking in the moment with my dogs. I said, "no but I will tell you in the morning."

Laying they're surrounded by my fur babies, in tears. I laid there in the kitchen and cuddled up with my dogs, hugging and holding them as tight as I could. And I thought about different moments in my life. Looking at the picture in my wallet of my nephews. Thinking about how they would miss me, what I would miss, all the special times still to be shared. Birthdays, anniversaries, Thanksgivings and Christmas'. And just spending sleepovers at the house getting pizza, watching movies.

Hearing Carter's infectious laugh wrestling in the living room, spending time at the pool. Or just playing video games having quiet dinners together. It wasn't fair to rob them or my family from that, nor my dogs or my friends. It was selfish in thinking, even though I was aching inside.

I took it as one short chapter in my life and then if I can learn to get through this. I can learn to get through anything. Although, I still deeply care for her, and learned to forgive. I did learn one of the early lessons in life. If you love something, you have to learn to let it go. And if it comes back, then it's meant to be.

And it's hard to do that when you're married, when you make a bond with God, your family, your wife. It's something truly different when you put that ring around your finger and place it on another. That symbol, that bond, and writing personal vows to her that I honored. It's hard to move on, it's hard to not give up, but you have to learn to love yourself enough, that sometimes you have to let go. Not to let somebody hurt you so deeply anymore. To continue to hurt you, challenging the person you know you are inside, and who you're meant to be.

I turned on the shower, sitting in the bottom of the tub and letting soft, warm water pour over me, it calms me. And it made the pain feel like it washed away, even if just for a brief moment. Crying out with a deep crushing pain over my heart and chest. A hole in my chest.

Then I guess that's why I've always been drawn to bodies of water. How they seem to relax me in thoughts and feelings. Slowing life down just for a brief few moments, reflecting on life, a deep breath and reflecting on the things that really do matter.

How water reacts to admiration. The studies conducted by Dr. Masaru Emoto they've taken water and sealed it in airtight acrylic containers with speakers outside. One of the water sealed containers was fed nothing, but negativity thoughts and words. And the other was fed nothing but positivity and good thoughts.

By the end of the study, the water under a microscope showed huge visible differences. The one that receive negativity became cloudy, bacteria buildup in it, contaminated and dirty. The water that received positivity during the study became purified, crisp and clean. Under the microscope, it looked like little snowflake crystals that form from the purity of it. So, if that tells you anything your mind, your body, your soul and our capabilities on what is possible.

From there I headed to the living room to cuddle with my dogs up on our futon in the living room. Made some popcorn we shared, watched a movie and tried to get some good rest for tomorrow. The next morning still feeling loss, I almost felt like my wife at the time had died. The person I married wasn't the person the one that I know today. I loved her enough to be able to fight through it all. All the madness and arguments over the smallest things. Fighting for things that she wanted and dreamed about and I'm proud of that. But even in the end, sadly I could never be enough, so I had to learn to work on me.

I went to work the next morning, going straight to my office, going through emails and then just emotion starts hitting me. Nothing in particular caused it, just a smack in the face. Realizing that I'm losing her and losing everything. Because I always had thoughts that once I got married that was it. That I found the one and I'd never be alone, happy and I guess still a part of me will always feel this way. But eight a.m. rolls around, and Mr. Bill White came into my office, shut the door to ask, "so what's going on." And that's when I proceeded to fight back the tears and tell him somewhat of what has been happening between me and my wife. He kind of knew, since she was missing company events and functions. Plus, when asked, I would brush it off and move on to another subject.

After getting a brief description of what was going on. How she wasn't coming home, how she wasn't respecting me in my feelings, spending money non-stop and acting out. He asked if I could if he could pray with me. I said "yes, of course…I really need to."

We prayed for myself, for the dogs, for my family, for her family and lastly for her. And then from that moment we immediately left work and went down a couple of blocks from the office in Lagrange Kentucky. And we met with a couple that worked at a local church. From that, giving them a brief description tell them what I was currently facing with my spouse in our marriage, where nothing seems to work. No matter how much I give, I don't get anything in return other than sadness, and I'm just not happy, I'm just falling apart.

They turn me on to a book Christian lead called marriage 911. From this book, it gives you details each week to work on yourself and not focus on your spouse. Especially one that's not willing to go to therapy, someone not willing to listen to your thoughts and feelings. Not willing to work on the relationship at all and have pretty much just cashed out.

Each day you read portions of the book, Bible verses that help with relationships. Worksheets and exercises that pretty much have you focus on yourself. Your needs to be a better person rather than lower your thinking. Why is this person doing this, why don't they love me anymore, was it something I did?

They switch your form of thinking, to focus on yourself, your wants and needs. What deep down makes you happy? And this is kind of where I got the idea to start doing a bucket list. For myself, things I've always wanted to do and just have never done. What are the reasons she became controlling about a year-and-a-half to two years into our relationship when we started having all these problems? We stopped having fun, sharing adventures, feelings of happiness and joy. And I think part of that is because she was losing control of the person she created and the person she was starting to become.

But at the time I didn't know that, and I had to learn that through stages and steps. But it all seemed to somewhat make sense towards the end of the relationship, towards the end of our marriage. And honestly writing this book I hope to look back now, that she's better. I know I've become a better person, but it's a drive each day to move forward to do so. When you climb out of your darkest moments, the pit of Hell, you have to. You have to build momentum in happiness and continue looking towards what's next. The best is yet to come. And I hope that she's happy and that she receives everything she's ever wanted. That's all I ever wanted for her.

Because at the time when we were having all these issues, she was sporadic, her anxiety was through the roof. Yelling, screaming, fighting for no reason. No remorse, no feeling, no love. It was just a cover for how she felt internally and what she was doing outside of our marriage. And deep down I knew what was going on, what she was doing but when you're in that situation you try to cover it up. You're ashamed, you're embarrassed, and you try with all your heart to love that person back. Back to the way things were in the beginning.

You look in the mirror and question yourself. You don't understand why they would do the things that they do, and you want to make it better. You want to go back to how things were before; you don't want it to end. You don't want to fail your commitment to her, yourself....to love. But sometimes, there can be no reasoning and you have to learn to quit beating yourself up for things that you cannot control.

So, from this, I began a bucket list. Things she would never let me do once she became controlling over my life, and she could no longer control her own anymore. I began right away, where I wrote down I believe in a half hour, 70 plus things that I've always wanted to do. Some of them are personal goals, places to visit, just different things I wanted to do with my life.

The cool thing about a bucket list is it's personal; it's yours, it's whatever you feel that makes you happy. And it was a number one thing that helped me realize that there is a lot of life left to live. Things I have yet to accomplish, to help me get through this horrible time. That's one thing I learned from the marriage 911 course is that you need to learn to make yourself happy. You need to move on from what makes you sad even though it's the person you may have once loved; you need to get back to being happy like when you first met. If not, there is no chance that this person will ever come back to your heart.

From this I started doing things that I love to do, I started writing more. I started reading more books; I started watching more movies and comedies. I started working out again. I started getting involved in myself, around nature. Being outside noticing little things, like birds everything. But once I started noticing my self-esteem from being beat down and torn apart. That I was a horrible person even though it wasn't the description of me I was given from her. But in reality, it was a reflection of herself. A lot of times people that love one another feel like they have to harm the one closest to them, when they have no other outlet of themselves.

So, from that, I began this journey which I'm still currently on. And the crazy thing is I started having other people, that I had no idea they were having issues in their marriage and relationships start reaching out to me. Ask him why you are so happy like what would have you done that's different what have you done that's different from me. Just currently at the time, I was working 7 days a week I was losing my house my dream home 40-acre log cabin wrap around porch no neighbors within three-quarters of a mile.

Something I talked with my mother the day before she passed away. I talk to her about this dream I had. Something I dreamed about as a kid. About having a log cabin, wrap around porch, no neighbors and at that time I never thought I'd get to that point. Where I could have it, and at the same time she received some money from a class action lawsuit off of medication that gave her sugar diabetes.

Now my dad being the realest that he is, did not believe that she would ever receive any money. And I and my grandmother took her and told her to talk to these lawyers. "Go for it if you think you can get it, go for it." "no harm is going to be done." "It wasn't your fault, that you got diabetes." "You didn't ask for this."

And on the day, she received $80,000 check after the lawyer fees, we showed it first to my dad. And from this, me and my mother were big movie buffs. We love watching movies all the time, always up for enjoying a great story. And she wanted to invest some of this money into a local Drive-In on the Eastside of Cincinnati. She always took us there at least once a summer as a family to watch movies. But I still cherish these memories, but I told her not to. The reason why is I always had a vision of buying a farm and having a drive-in theater on it. Overlooking a lake and just being a serene setting, all her own.

Not to this day, that is yet to happen. I was very close, but circumstances change, situations change and apparently hearts change as well. What you want is not always in your control I still have that dream, and I'm very good at achieving my dreams. My mom was a big dreamer which kind of balanced us out. My dad being the realist, a little better the last couple years. My dad is learning and has started to realize some of his dreams and goals himself. And after that, I want to say dad I'm proud of you.

I miss my mom very much. There's not a day that goes by that I don't think of her. She's the best mother anyone could ever wish to have.

Providing more love to her children, listening to each one of our dreams and pushing them emotionally chasing those dreams. What we lacked financially, our family made up with love and the closeness we all have. We can always talk about anything together, having great family traditions that I'm eternally thankful for. Thanksgiving at my grandmother's, baking Christmas cookies as a group, banging pots and pans out on my grandmother's porch at New Year's watching the ball drop. Drinking my mom's punch and watching Dick Clark on a TV screen. New and old traditions that I know she's smiling down at my brothers and sisters that have continued those on today.

C. Stanton

Ch. 12. A Chance to Start Over

"Success is a pleasure. If you're not satisfied and fulfilled with what you're doing today. You can never become successful."

—Abraham Lincoln

A chance to find myself again, to renew and take form of something better. A life more beautiful than before, coming out from darkness to transform in the light. A life more vibrant and full of more color than ever before. And so, I began moving forward, taking steps.

After some time, some hard struggles and going through my divorce. Being sick and losing my job, my dream home having to go back home. And I realized that might have been the best thing to happen. Spending much-needed time around family and friends. Spending those last few weeks with my beloved grandma. I still miss our times watching UK Basketball together. One of my fondest memories was the Wildcats making it to the final four in 2014.

Taking some time as her health was fading to drive home on the weekend and watch the games together. Knowing if they were able to make it to the championship game that it would be on the following Monday. Now I already had it in my head that I would make the return trip to watch the game but as they made it one step closer to another title. I led on that I would have to work and wouldn't be able to catch the game. Knowing good and well I was going to watch it with her. She said, "Oh Hun, I know you have to work." "It's ok you can call me throughout the game." I said "Grandma, they are working me long hours and I doubt I'll be able to watch the game or step away to call." Knowing I already had a plan to work just the normal shift, but I had to sell it.

She said as she always did in her little voice. "Oh, that's ok Clint. If you can't I understand, they'll always be another game." But I decided to leave work early that Monday, to drive home to spend the game with her. Because we never really know when the last time....is the last time. And unfortunately, this was....

About midway through my trip, I called to let her know I was held up at work and unfortunately wouldn't be able to make it. But that I would call her at halftime. Knowing good and well that I was going to drive up and surprise her with her favorite pizza, Donato's thin crust founders. The same pizza I use to sneak with my mom from her when we would spend the day watching new movies. We only did it as my mom had health problems and she was afraid grandma would get on her.

Now my grandma later told me, she wouldn't have, especially knowing how delicious this pizza was. But my last memory of us watching UK play was a gift. Calling ahead to have it ready to go, parking down from her living room window off the street, so not to ruin my surprise. Ringing her doorbell and seeing the look of both happiness and surprise on her face.... priceless.

Although I'm not sure which, if it was for me or for the pizza. But no matter, bringing her a little bit of joy, a smile, a nice surprise and a great basketball game to follow. None the less, we fell to the superior guard play of the eventual champions the Connecticut Huskies. The day was amazing and spending time together, as we've done so many times before. Little moments, that mean so much. That's what life is about, capturing those little moments. So, blessed to have that memory and to have spent that time with her. Not knowing that in a few months you would be gone and as fate has it, I would be in Lexington. Home of Wildcats Basketball.

Finalizing my divorce and dealing with having you laying in a hospital bed. It was really tough on me emotionally; it was just really hard to visit you in a place that wasn't your home. And our talks, try to keep a positive outlook on things at this time was very rough. But still surprising you and the nursing staff when they would call telling me you were not eating. Then I would show up with your go to meals. Donato's founder's pizza, crackle barrel, white castles or gold stars cheese coneys.

Seeing her smile bringing her favorites in, having our special talks together. It was just really tough to see her struggling. Grabbing my hands and mentioning how much I look like my grandfather. Placing her hands over top of mine and how much she misses him and my mom. And then I remember having that talk, and you saying, "Clint I'm just really tired." "Struggling to breathe and not being able to do much." I want you kids to take care of one another." "I'm ready to go home." But you weren't talking about going home to your house you were talking about going home to them up in heaven.

I remember wiping away the tears and you holding my hands having our special talks. And I said, "Grandma, if you feel that way you need to go." It wasn't that I wanted her to go, there could be nothing so much farther from the truth. I could just tell in her voice and see it in her eyes. But she was just physically tired and was ready to move on to her next chapter. "I miss Curt, and I miss your Mom."

And I told her "Grandma we will be fine, we'll come together as a family like we've always done, and we'll be fine." And I couldn't help it, I tried to hold back the tears, but there was no holding back. I cried mostly sad tears and also a few happy ones. We as a family all knew how much she struggled since the day my mom left. Just breathing on a day-to-day basis and being weak. Not able to live her life the way she wanted, on her terms. I know deep down she was ready to go.

And still, to this day, the day they took her and announced she was going into hospice. I remember being out in the hallway with my brothers and sisters and we're all shedding tears to the hospital floor. I'm just seeing the smile on her face, and she's telling us it will all be okay. In that moment the oddest thing happened that when she seen me coming out of the room getting wheeled out to the hallway. Ready to be transported to the ambulance. She gives me a huge smile and a five.

Again, shedding more tears but stuck in a difficult, weird place. Those of sadness and of happiness. All us kids were stuck in this weird place of crying, joy, and laughter all at the same time. She wasn't fearful, not one bit and gave us some comfort in showing it. Knowing she is heading home to see loved ones that she's so deeply missed over the years. One without pain. I think then we all couldn't help but take the news a little easier. Seeing you smile in that moment. One without fear, welcoming this new page in your story.

Angel Among Us

Nearing halloween 2014- my favorite time of year. The leaves changing, the air is crisp. Staying up the night before a family is gathered around in your room. I just didn't want you to pass in your sleep with no one there to hold your hand, to talk and let you go to the other side. I believe everyone felt the same way. The doctors describing that your breathing will slow, your oxygen levels will lower, and you will eventually pass, just going to sleep. As the time got near, the doctors said" you would no longer respond, or wake from anything." But as life often tells us, life and its moments cannot always be explained. The time was near, but my favorite picture of you laying by your bedside.

Of you and your husband, my grandfather Curtis Mobley on your front porch swing laughing hysterically. I'm not sure who captured this timeless moment, but I am truly grateful for it, as I'm sure my family would agree. Showing only joy, and love, no pain. I reached for the Photo, and in that moment, you awoke and looked directly at me and the photo. Then we all reached for your hand, talking to let you that we are all here with you and that it was ok to go.

Such a strong person, even in that moment, all of us saying our last goodbyes. I still felt like you were holding on. I couldn't take it anymore, and felt I had to leave the room as you closed your eyes. Walking the hall, in my mind having our special talks again, letting you have one last goodbye with everyone. And in my heart, I felt when I returned you would go. And sure enough, you were gone.

Talking outside with my dad, brothers and sisters. The sun was shining; the air was warm on our skin recalling great memories you brought to us all. A group of three to four white butterflies bounced flower to flower, then around us as a group before disappearing in the sky. All of us looking at one another with a slight smile.

It was no secret she was a huge UK Wildcats basketball fan and I remember growing up as a kid just south of Cincinnati. My dad being a Bearcats fan, but I remember once we moved from Cincinnati to Florence. We had some bearcat attire on coming into grandma's kitchen at 5 years old. My grandma, being grandma the die-hard Wildcats fan she was and bleeding blue to her core.

She always told this story best saying it with a smile. "Any of my grandsons coming in this house they have to be a Wildcats fan." And another thing, "The next time you come to visit your grandma, you better have Kentucky blue on."

Ch. 13. A City of Blue

"A successful person never loses…They either win or learn!"

—John Calipari

So, there I found my true love for Wildcats basketball. And now as fate has it, taking a new job in Lexington Kentucky and starting my life over again. Taking small steps moving forward, moving on without her. Some steps are just writing goals down. Personal goals, dreams for myself and others. For the day, and for the week and then for the month I began physically writing them down. Before you know it, you have goals written down for a powerful year.

One so I could see them, you have to see your dreams first before you can chase them. Be very specific about your goals and what you want, and a time frame you want to achieve them. Keep these notes on you in your wallet and look at them periodically throughout the day. At the start of the day and before you close your eyes at night, visualize yourself already with those dreams. Believe.

Creating a vision board is a great tool, as it also helps as well and for those of you who don't know what it is. Basically visualizing what you want, cutting items out of magazines placing them as a collage on a backboard. When you visually see that every morning when you wake up and look at it before you go to sleep at night. You trigger your brain towards getting those things and what you want. It may come in unconventional ways but with an open mind. Life I believe tries to work in favor of you and your dreams.

I started using these principles after my divorce. And moments leading up to the final weeks and days. I truly learned to love myself, her and to let her make her own decisions. That if you truly love something, you have to learn to let it go. You have to learn to forgive, if you don't you can't grow, holding a grudge. Holding pain in your heart, affects your whole life. More importantly, you have to learn to love yourself as well.

Free will. That if thru it all, if it was ever meant to be it will come back to you. And even at one point, she did. She wanted to come home and work on things. I couldn't believe it after all this time, a year and a half of struggling to make things like they once were. For her to love me again, to come after all this past time took courage from both of us. What I found, was once I stopped focusing on her and worked on myself.

Things that truly made myself happy. And this thinking became a part of life, happiness in knowing. You can only control your own thoughts and decisions. No matter how much you want something, you cannot control it; you can't force it. You can only control your own thoughts, decisions and your mind. Once you discover this, life, when it is at its most challenging moments, becomes easier. Keep your head up to the stars and never stop fighting for what you want in your heart. And so, I did, in a town ruled by Wildcat blue.

I've been here in town for a couple of months now, working trying to pick up the pieces. Moving forward in a positive ray of light, moving to a new place. Taking on a new job, Lexington being the place where life was taking me in this next venture. A time to heal, thinking of my grandmother and all the wonderful memories we shared together.

The city no matter where I went, made me think of her. I had my struggles, but one thing was for certain. Watching each game, made me feel closer to her.

Bringing up memories as a kid. I remember seeing my first live UK game. An exhibition only but it didn't matter. I and my older brother Shane got to go see them play at US Bank Arena in Cincinnati. The great Rex Chapman and Johnny Locke. Man was I excited to hear that they were coming to town to play. Just the four of us, with my grandma and grandpa. Directly behind one of the baskets, looking down with popcorn, hotdogs, soda and cotton candy in our tummy's. How those memories and those times still stay with me now.

Full circle in a city surrounded by Wildcat blue. An amazing feeling in a time, when it was much needed. Funny how life works out in mysterious ways. Scents, sounds and small visuals bring back extraordinary memories and moments in time.

I was blessed enough to live out another one of my bucket items. Receiving free tickets to my first game at Rupp Arena...the first without my grandma being around. It was hard being here in town all season, catching myself wanting to call her on the phone or sitting in the living room with Donato's pizza and enjoy the games. It was actually quite difficult to even watch a full game, as I constantly thought about our times together cheering them on. I loved those moments and keep them in my heart always.

I thought back when I was first telling her about my bucket list idea after my divorce, of going to a game at

C. Stanton

Rupp around my birthday. It's a tradition I have started every year since, to honor her and her memory. This is shortly after I shared my skydiving video with her in her living room, not letting her know that I was taking down my number #1 item till after the fact. As she would have been so worried the whole time.

But not as worried as my sister's became, once my battery died midday and they could not get ahold of me. My brother's being brothers, included them in a group text sending funny gif images back and forth of my skydiving demise. The truly funny thing looking back now, is we

had to wait all day for that moment to leap from the plane. I know who does this, who jumps from a perfectly good airplane.

Apparently, a lot of people. Young, old it didn't matter when we got to the airfield. My friend Tara terrified of what was ahead. And rain, low lying clouds in the area forced us to wait. Trying to schedule it for another time. So being on hold for a couple of hours, decided to get some lunch…..and maybe a beer or two…. then a few shots…. I can't really say 😊 but let's just say we made it a fun filled day, and with her new-found courage we pushed forward and faced the challenge ahead.

Still jokingly wanting to back out at this point, knowing in her mind she was going to go thru with it. She had to. Skies were clear, and we could see planes and parachutes in the air as we pulled up. Still terrified but smiling all the way. Our names were called, as we quickly suited up for the jump. Tara jumping up and down nervously, as we walk out of the hanger towards the plane. "Are you sure you still want to do this?" she said. And all I said, was "look, do you see anyone on the ground not smiling." She said, "All right Mr. Stanton, let's do this!" lol. Too funny, but what an amazing, freeing experience. I would recommend it to anyone who has the chance.

Once you get past your initial fear, and you free from the plane. You feel like you're flying, like a bird. No worries and carefree. Now, I love roller coasters, and that was my biggest thought. That it was going to be the greatest roller coaster ever, then after this, no coaster could compare.

Boy, was I mistaken. They could not be two totally different feelings. That feeling, that tickle in your stomach going thru the first drop of a coaster. Skydiving, no feeling other than that of flight, like a bird...freeing. The most freeing experience I've ever had in my life, and probably the most amazing...

Achieving my number 1 and number 2 on my list all at once. To go skydiving and to touch a cloud. To feel one step closer to the clouds, the heavens above and lastly, but not least....my mom....

C. Stanton

Ch. 14. Accident is the Mother of Invention

"There are no accidents... there is only some purpose that we haven't yet understood."

— Deepak Chopra

I couldn't really use my Jeep to move my furniture from one place to the next. So, I asked to borrow my mother's old dodge van. Moving from one edge of town to the other. I picked up a nice new 5 drawer dresser a few days ago, beautiful cherry wood, loaded in the back. Stacked to the rim with clothes and ready to move across town to the new place.

January 31st, 2017, a Tuesday night. Just like any other, peaceful with a few clouds laying in the sky nestled around the moon. I decided I wanted to watch the Wildcats game tonight at a new local restaurant close to downtown. It wasn't, but 7 or 8 miles from my new place and I left a little early, so I could order some food to snack on before the game started. It's 15min past eight, just a few blocks from my destination. Sitting quietly in front of Transylvania college at a local crosswalk and a couple of students started to venture across the four-lanes of traffic to and from class.

The next thing I know is I'm in severe pain getting hit from behind and my car lifting up in the air and then slamming back to the ground. I had never been hit this hard in my life. But a weird thing happened. At this moment, I felt like I was moving at such a high rate of speed, then it slowed. Almost like in slow motion when I first got hit as I'm moving forward, almost as if I was put in a bubble. Time and everything slowed

down inside the car. Things are getting tossed around in every direction. As my head went forward, then to the back of my seat. Things quickly sped back up and then I came to a violent stop.

My back and my neck were in severe pain, hitting the front of my windshield, although having my seat belt on as I'm just really tall. Thanks, dad. Lol. I'm 6 ft 5, so it didn't seem to help too much from my forehead, wanting to make sweet, sweet contact with the windshield glass. At least it wasn't my face, as I would at most like to keep that part intact. Leaning forward I smacked my head on the top of the windshield and that did not feel the greatest.

Keep in mind that a new president had just been elected to office. It maybe was just me being concussed, as all I can remember is a student running over to my driver side door. Smoke all around the outside of the car, knocked on the driver side window, and the glass falling down inside the door. As he asked if I was okay. I said "I think so" because at this moment I'm looking all over my shoulder in a panic, thru the side mirrors for rioters in the street. Cops and tear gas, all that jazz. I actually thought a grenade launcher hit the back of the van with how hard I was hit from behind. Ready to exit the vehicle full Schwarzenegger style in some late 80s, early 90s action classic. "Get to tha Choppa!!!" Taking on a band of terrorist in a threat for survival, while saving the beautiful woman lead of the film in the process. Yea, none of this was to be the case, well at least on this day,... wink. 😊

The impact though left my brand new 5 drawer dresser exploded on the inside of the car, a powder of wood dust particles and broken latch handles against the dash. Anything and everything that was inside of it was thrown all about, looking like a tornado ravished this thing. Luckily

it hit the back of the seat, but I still can't to this day confirm. Still I'm kind of out of it at this point, not sure what was going on. But my second thought was of the person that hit me after the student came up to my window, hoping they're alright.

Wondering still, what happened... Me, confused... "Soooo.... what happened, terrorist?" Confused face from student, "Ummm, no....???? A full-size truck just rear end you at about 70". "Ohhh....? That explains it I guess then." Getting out groggy from the impact and not full Arnold mode, I walk back to the rear of the vehicle, making sure that everyone involved was okay.

There were no warnings, no screeching of tires, brakes or smoke. One minute you're at a crosswalk looking forward at life. The next your hit from behind, in pain with no warning. That's just how life is. It's a journey, and you can be making all the right choices. Then bam!!! It's just that kind of planet. But how we pick ourselves up, pick up the pieces, that's what makes the difference. What I found out after exiting our vehicle's and now seeing the aftermath of a full-size Chevy truck hitting the van, colliding with mine. Lights glaring back at me, a distraught young brunette walking towards me. Tears in her eyes and physically upset. What I didn't know was at that present moment, her husband was getting flown to U.K.

Hospital and was in need of a liver transplant. She was racing, emotional distraught, driving the 3 + hours away from her home in Pikeville to try and make it to the hospital before he passed away.

At this point, my head, my back, my neck felt insignificant. I told her "As long as you're okay, I'm okay." We hugged and talked about life, what she was dealing with waiting for the authorities to arrive. And how we

can hurry this along with officers once they get here, so she can be by his side. After 45 grueling minutes and her getting permission from authorities to leave she was able to by his side. Somehow driving her crippled truck, the block and a half down the street to the hospital.

After my statements the police officer asked me where I was headed and that he would take me if I needed a lift. As my mom's vehicle was undrivable. Motor mounts cracked, antifreeze, gas and oil laying all in the street. This ride was definitely done for, for sure. I was headed to a new micro brewery restaurant near downtown that had just opened for a nice dinner and to watch the Wildcats play.

It wasn't exactly as I planned it, being in the back of a cruiser pulling up to the bar. Which I'm sure I received some funny looks but for a only for a short time. But I was able to watch the game, thinking of my grandmother, trying to drown out the pain with a couple brew haus. And even the bartender was happy to obliqe buying me a shot at halftime to help dull out the pain. Great food and some good beers, the back and head pain subsided for a brief moment.

Smiling bringing back memories with my grandma, spending time together watching Wildcat games.

Angel Among Us

Remembering just a year prior going to my first game in Rupp Area. Sitting in the second to last row up in the rafters to a packed house on senior night. But the whole night, an empty seat stayed next to me. I kept telling her at the hospital that I always wanted to go to a game at Rupp. And I believe she was there right beside me all this time, watching it together. A tradition I started for myself, that every year towards the end of the season, around my birthday in March that I would go to a game in honor of you Grandma.

I'm not quite sure why in this moment, it triggered this memory, but it did.

That night, once I had the wreck, I asked my friend Matt from work if I could get a ride with him in the morning if I was able. Now, most people would think it was even crazy to attempt such a thing just a few hours after being in a bad wreck. But what I didn't tell you is at my current position, I was questioned my commitment and work ethic. All because of a dream I'm fulfilling now. A writer, a singer, and now an author. I was asked to show more commitment towards my job, then of my singing or writing career.

Now in life were often questioned or pushed away from our dreams, hopes and wishes. Never let a person, job or even one with a roller coast outlook and bald head, anything or anyone ever take this from you. No matter what, stand up for what you believe in, what your heart tells you and of what you want. Never let go of this. I proudly stood my ground, never letting any of my outside influences affect my work. I looked him straight in the eye after his, "I'm a straight shooter speech," lol. My response, chest stuck out at this time, leaning in forward, ready in my head to flip over his desk in front of him with a

Schwarzenegger growl, that is evident in every movie. Come to think of it, "I'll be back, "Come with me if you want to live," Girawlll!!!!"

But I didn't, I didn't let this one person affect my thoughts on my work. Much less than outside of it. I don't live to work, although I will give a 110% but at some point, you have to have balance in everything you do. If not, any one piece will start to crumble and fall apart around you. Just like anything else, you are only as strong as your weakest link. So intently looking back at him across his desk, here is my actual response.

"I'm shocked that you would even ask me about my job commitment in question." "I come in 30min to an hour before yourself and stay 30min to an hour after you leave". "But to bring up my personal life, dreams outside of here I don't know how to take it." "Other than, I'm also a straight shooter, and would never question what people, including yourself, your dreams and or what you outside of this place." "But no job, no amount of money, no person will ever keep me from my dreams, sorry."

Boom! Drop the mic. But that's what you have to do, when for no reason. Your character, lively hood, and dreams are brought in to question. No matter what, you fight for what you believe is right and what you believe in.

So even though I was in a wreck the night before, though I'm in severe pain, hobbling to his car and now not able to speak. Neck and face swollen from the whiplash. I went in to work. To prove a point.

For a total of 93 min before I was in so much pain, I could no longer take it. I was in tears but know one thing when some tells you; you can't do something. You have to try.

I went home 5 minutes down the road, bed ridden, not being able to move. Not to mention I could not get comfortable to save my life. It was terrible, not knowing if I was going to lose my voice. If I'd be the same singer, I was before the accident. If my back was ever going to get back to normal.

Sometimes in life, situations are just taken out of our control. You may not see the miraculous beauty or the direction of the journey you're going in but the universe, our creator, has a greater plan. It's with grace in perspective that we can truly take a step back and at our worst times of need and pain. We are given just what we need, what we have sought after.

Maybe a chance meeting, something that pushes you down the road of life, a year, a decade. Half a lifetime, sit back, enjoy it and actually witness the beauty in it all. I think we're all giving a gift to share with the world. It's how we use our gift, how we fight and struggle for that dream that makes us all unique and different. I believe this makes the world a better place, what we're here for. And even after this wreck lying in bed try to make to make sense of it all. Being at work for those couple of minutes. I knew that I couldn't do it, in severe pain. My face, my neck, everything is all swollen. I can't hardly talk, my back, my neck hurting and all I'm doing is sitting in a cubicle working on the computer, and I couldn't even do that.

Just a day before my boss brought up my commitment to my job. That I need to be more committed to work, than my commitment to my music or my writing and said I'm a straight shooter. And I'm proud of how I responded to that all. Although, I was very angry none of this stuff ever took away from my job or my prior commitments. I was never late always worked over I looked in his face and I said "I'm a straight shooter too, and no job and no amount of money will ever take me away from my dream of writing, my dream as a singer or author it doesn't affect my job and I won't let you or a family member or a friend ever take that away sorry this is not going to happen."

And when I went back home lying in bed, I decide to finally take the work clothes off that I struggle to even get my shoes on and tie my shoelaces earlier that morning. I went to the restroom, and I looked in the mirror and all I could see was a Lynyrd Skynyrd shirt. An Old vintage Lynyrd Skynyrd shirt I just liked it because of the eagle design on the front of it and the colors. A blue shirt with red, white blue throughout the whole design but what I thought about was my mom when I bought it years ago.

She always liked to hear me sing Lynyrd Skynyrd's song Simple Man. And then again in that moment, I felt like she was with me thru everything. Protecting me even beyond death but she is still doing that for all her children. And I talked to my dad to let him know what was going on but that I was ok.

For two and a half weeks I laid there, and I couldn't do anything. I didn't have a vehicle, so I decided to instead of him driving down all the way south to Lexington to get me and taking me all way back once I was able to go back to work. I figured I would take an Uber back to Florence, try to relax in the car, get up there and spend time with my dogs, my dad and my family.

Relaxing on the couch and soaking in the tub constantly, I guess it was a couple of days later I met a friend for lunch. And once I was done eating, I was searching for my debit card to pay. I couldn't find it anywhere, and I was thinking I must have left it at my dad's. I rushed home calling my dad along the way to see if it was laying out anywhere. It wasn't, and when I got there, I started looking through my wallet and could not find my debit card after I returned home. So, from there, I began pulling everything out of my wallet, ID card, my social security card, receipts different things of that nature laying it all out on a dresser in a back bedroom. That's when in the bottom pocket was a fortune cookie note with a fortune on it.

I had never seen this or recall this note, for I don't even know how it got in this corner pocket of my wallet. But what it said make me feel again like my mother was with me. "Accidents is the mother of invention." Now what I seen there was two words "accident" and "mother." I just couldn't believe it, I didn't know how else to take it, and again I'm shocked. Because I never put a fortune cookie note in my wallet before. And I do not recall this at all ever being in there or let alone the last time I had Chinese; I just don't even know how it got there.

But I feel like my mother was always around me. I felt it when I was in the wreck that there was just something protecting me, something keeping me from getting hurt worse than I was. And then I find this note showing up a few days later, and still I can't wrap my head around it. In life sometimes, we may not be able to understand or see things or fully understand how this life works. But our heart and feelings actually guide us towards our thoughts, towards what we feel is really going on.

Again, how my mother left us all notes on how to live our lives. How to treat one another and how we all felt a warm breeze or butterfly landing on your shoulder or finger was our mom. That a year later after her passing my grandmother and my dad presented a scrapbook of notes. Glittered scrapbook paper notes to us all individually, such a blessing and you could hear her voice coming thru the pages as we read those words on paper. My sister Amber's confirmed all of our thinking. It's just an amazing thing, the way things have transpired since you've been gone. That when you feel a warm breeze or a butterfly, landing on your shoulder or finger, "That's me saying Hi."

Losing our mom, how all of us kids have felt things in our heart and spirit, things that cannot be explained. So, I hope that telling the story through this writing, that if I can just reach one person or open one person's eyes. That things are not always as they seem, that you can shape a life the way you want it. You can chase dreams that seem unimaginable; you can truly do or be anything you want to be. And sometimes the journey is not the direction you wanted it to go, but it may be exactly where your life needs to lead.

But if you keep fighting, keep digging and you wake up every morning. Living, breathing your dreams, life will eventually open the doors for you to receive them. When life doesn't work out the way you want, and you're redirected. Keep an open mind to the possibilities this is what leads you to where you need to go; this is what leads you to your dreams.

My perspective on things now is what if the creator, what if God's whatever you believe is really protecting us from more hurt, more pain that we are not able to see. Maybe it's traffic, making you late for work or get to your destination on vacation. But what you can't see is maybe that's keeping you from a bad accident or meeting that particular person you're supposed to meet at that given time when you take a different route. Which causes you to go to a different gas station for coffee that you normally would not be at, and you meet the love of your life that morning. We really don't know?

Life Works in funny ways; it's how we keep our perspective and positive thinking that even when the bad comes, the worst of times. Take a deep breath, a step back and look towards what this event means. What can I learn from this, grow from it, and where is the good in it. It will be good hidden somewhere, because I think all things and all dreams we are meant to have and are naturally for the betterment of our existence.

We all have separate dreams, we all have different wishes, exceptional goals and were put here for a reason. Look at it, asking three questions and challenge yourself differently. "What do I want, how hard am I willing to work to get, and what are the teachings behind it? What I'm going to learn going through these challenges and grow?" With this adversity, what's the beautiful story on the tail end. On the other side of it.

That's how I try to look at it now with my perspective on things, going through one of the roughest times of my life and then just setting goals.

Chasing dreams, you know you only fail when you stop going after them. It doesn't have a time frame, when you fail to stop chasing these dreams. That's when your dream dies.

Do this for me, don't let them die. Just keep climbing, keep digging, keep fighting and you'll get them. And your life tends to become more cheerful and happy, taking the colors of life in a totally different way. Stop to take a moment and soak it in because we don't know when the last time you'll see these simple things that makes life so grand, so spectacular. A rainbow and sunset, whatever reaches your heart; whatever it takes to get you in the right mindset, the right perspective forging you towards what you need.

And I believe the timing of my accident it was, just after losing my grandmother, my divorce about a year after and then losing my job. Getting offered another one but having a boss who questioned my dreams. Telling me I can't grow, I can't chase my dreams outside of work. I can't do certain things and then having the courage to stand up for what I truly believe in. To fight for them and for my heart.

I look back now, and I'm extremely proud that I did stand up. That I wouldn't let anybody take away my thoughts, my dreams and goals. And if they did take away my job, there's always another job out there. There's always other money you can make, other directions you can take but don't let someone ever take your thoughts, your heart, your soul about what you truly believe that you are.

Faith is granting the substance of evidence not yet seen. I'm not sure what struggles you're going through, what hardships you may be facing. What you're seeking in this game we call life but always have faith. Faith in your family, yourself, friends and faith in the creator of all things. There is a purpose.

Always keep faith, never give up. Even after this wreck and I couldn't talk for six to seven weeks, couldn't sing and couldn't do a lot of the things I truly love. I felt like my dreams of being a singer and doing the things with my music, that I love to do up on stage it was getting taken away from me. What this event brought about was perspective, the greater appreciation of the gifts I was given. Writing to heal, to learn from life's experiences, to listen people stories. How we all are here; how lucky we are of the opportunity we have been given. I hope in reading that I give some different perspective and insight on things that I've went through. Going through my hardships, my divorce, losing my mom, my grandmother, my dream house. We have all lost something; it's just a part of life. You have a choice to always bounce back.

That I wanted to show perspective, I wanted to show there's things in this life that can't be explained, things that happen out of our control. That if you truly feel like something's there, believe it. I still feel like my mother is around, watching over my family…then in reality they are.

Trust me, understand that thoughts manifest things. Every dream began with a thought, with an idea, dreamed and visioned in your mind put together in place before it became true. Everything we see in this world was dreamed up before it was built, before it became a thing. You too can build your dreams in your mind, in your thoughts. And if you keep fighting, keep striving staying positive towards that dream it will come true.

That's just how the universe works. It may not come in the manner or the timing that you thought, but if you stay positive and keep striving, you can make all your dreams come true. You can be whatever you want. Rich beyond your wildest dreams, but wealth is not measured in money, but it's measured in what you give in the life you're given. What you're able to give to others, your community, family and friends. And I

believe mine is just this, what I'm living each day. The gift of song, the gift of lyrics, words and feelings put on paper to touch others. Trust what you're attracted to, your heart, it'll lead you where you need to go.

Whether it's books, music, art, whatever you're attracted to. Little signs will lead you where you need to go and what's your thoughts and dreams are. Just trust those feelings in your heart and in your mind and go for it don't let anything hold you back. When you get started, start with yourself first. Love yourself, all things, your dreams, everything you love and the universe it'll be returned back to you tenfold.

Endurance is the will to win...period. To do the small, daily disciplines towards your dreams. The little things in the background, the shadows. "To do the things, that others are not willing to do, to have the things others won't have." Jim Rohn. In life the more you give, the more you'll receive in return. And just with any relationship, it all starts with yourself, so if there's issues going on in your life where a relationship is not going the way you want. Issues at your job or during the course of days it seems like it's falling apart, that the sky is falling first look at yourself first. Then take the steps in your mind and actions to fix it.

Evaluate yourself what do I see that I want to change? What aspect or subtle changes can I make to move to the next level? And from what I found, to love one another, to love all things that you do yet know. But you first must learn to love yourself, evaluate yourself and what you truly want and eliminate things you don't.

If you don't love the job you're at change it, if you don't like a relationship or the direction you're going in change it. It all starts with you and how happy your life is on the inside, is directly reflective to how you make it on the outside. When you love yourself, other people, life will attract you to other situations, opportunities, and people want to be around you more, the universe works and shifts in your favor.

Same is true when you don't love yourself, when you see all things is negative, you attract more negativity. Sometimes life's detours ends up being the most beautiful point in our journey. Don't always look at the perspective of it being a bad thing, it may lead you to the love of your life or to a new promotion, or an investment opportunity anything and everything is possible. A new part of town or new restaurant or new scenic view. Embrace life's little detours, because if you. If you look at it as a positive thing, it can lead you to some of the most extraordinary experiences in this life.

Take your life to the next level reach for as far as you can reach. Take your potential as far as you can. If there's a skill you need to learn, learn it. If you can't learn the skill or don't have the ability or time, find someone who does, surround yourself with people that do. Surround yourself with those that have what you want, learn from them. Talk to them, anything you can do to get to where you need to go. Where you feel like you want to go, where you feel the world, the universe is taking you. That's your heart, that's your being. How you feel is what you're supposed to do. Have your hopes, your dreams; your ambition everything drive you. Always keep going for it, never stop no matter what, no matter how hard life kicks you down, stay positive in your mind and your heart. And pick yourself up, you deserve it.

One thing you learn when you're going through adversity, is if you find little ways to get past it. Close your eyes, breath slowly, deeply and let your mind take you to a place of calming gratitude. I've learned to meditate, to take 5-10 minutes a day sitting by the water, or a quiet place of your own, out in nature. Wherever you choose.

What I usually do is I find some body of water, I usually sit down and listen to the waves crashing against the shore, soaking in the sun. And think about what I truly want, what I love and what I am thankful for. Letting all pain, negative thoughts outside of my control subside.

You absolutely want to be specific in what you want, what you're asking. Give dates, details on what you want, how you're going to do it and keep it on you. Look at it 3 times a day morning, noon and night keep it in your thoughts and mind. Do not stop, period. Keeping your mind in the right state for what you want, and to keep you on the path to achieve them.

And every time negative thoughts comes in, another thing you can do in closing your eyes. Put both hands in the middle of your chest over your heart. Sit there and breathing slowly, breathe out deeply and think about what adversity am I hitting and how to get past it. What do I truly want, who is the person that I'm supposed to become and then slowly open your eyes. And think the next 17 seconds at a time, then on to 36 seconds then continue on and on and on till these thoughts have vanished.

Reflect on the greatness that you are, the positive aspects in your life. And every day when you keep thinking those thoughts, you keep striving for those dreams. You'll move forward inch by inch towards them. And then momentum starts to shift; you start coming closer and closer to your goals. A lot of people may not see it because a lot of people dreams have to happen in the background.

Why do people see sports athletes as great, God-given talent and this may be true but what they don't know is. They work hundreds and hundreds of hours inside the gym alone. Under the stadium lights catching footballs, tossing a baseball, shooting free throws for that one shining moment when they're supposed to show their greatness. It's being prepared, looking towards your dreams and saying how can I get

there? What do I need to do to be better today, than I did yesterday? Failing to prepare, is preparing to fail.

What drives you, how can I become better, how can I help my fellow person, how can I help my family, friends, and community? That is purpose. It may not always be what is in our personal goals. But the goals that we create to help others and help the world around us. That's what makes us all special. Jack Canfield has a Formula E equals R equals O. Case in point is E equals events R equals response and O equals outcome.

What is your outcome, in everything you do from start at the end? What do you ultimately want from this outcome? We all have events that happen to us in life. Some good, some bad, some extraordinary, some out of ordinary but it's all perspective. How much we love ourselves and those around us. Trying to understand these events and what is our response? Learning from these, and the outcome that we need to give.

Now I'm not perfect but I'm learning, and I hope you're learning as well. That your outlook on life, perspective and how things really are. You can make it what you. In life, we can't stop the events that come into our life. Some we can, but usually the hard, challenging, unwanted one's we cannot. But the happiness inside yourself, grateful for the opportunities and the life you have been giving. You shape your emotions and control the state that you're in. That when life's hardships and challenges hit, your state will shape your response. What am I to learn and grow from this? And what is the outcome that I wish to have at the end of this? What do you want?

You can manifest it to make it happen. Strive to be happy on every occasion, no matter how bad it is you can twist and find a silver lining. What's the meaning behind all this? What I am I to learn, to grow

from? These events are supposed to make you stronger, to make you better, to make you more adaptable to the rights and wrongs of the world.

Trust your heart, trust your feelings and if I can leave you with one more thing. Again, you can take it how it is, but I know with what I witnessed. Some amazing things that this world has to offer. What I've experienced in my life the last couple of years, things hard to believe to be true, to be possible. That what we feel and what we know. What we see are two different things. That your heart and your faith is what shapes your life. I know my mom is still around us all.

Surrounding my brothers and sisters. Amber, Autumn, Shane, Adam, my little niece Ashlee and my nephews Hunter, Andrew, Carter, Ethan and Franklin. Still there with my grandmother, my grandfather, they're together, still around us all. And from what I experienced in November of 2017 in Cocoa Beach.... it is no different.

Something I've been waiting for in my heart for 10 years. To show me a sign, to show me something extraordinary. That life as we know it, in this one and the next. That those we love are still here, still connected... is an absolutely amazing thing.

Ch. 15. Lessons to Live by

"Do something you're passionate about. Find your calling and chase it."

—Anonymous

"It's not important how long you live, but how you live."

—Jim Rohn

One of the things that I learned was to ask for help, never to feel ashamed enough not to. I had a couple of books along the way that helped me as well, and I did a few things outside of those that help to get me through this difficult time I want to share.

It's crazy to say that I can't determine which was a more difficult time. The shocking loss of my mother talking to her the night before with no warning and then her being gone. Or loving someone so much, fixing a marriage and trying to make a life together with someone and them not loving you back, no matter what you did. No matter how far you're willing to go to show her that you care. About her and her dreams and thru it all that you loved her.

Praying, asking for help I was introduced to a book called marriage 911. And it's a Christian led book. But the basics of this book is it was created by a couple that were going through a difficult time, and one of the spouses was not willing to work with the other on repairing the relationship. The basic takes bits and pieces out of the Bible that speaks of marriage, honoring each other and tells you how to address certain issues that you may be facing.

And one of those issues is learning to love yourself first, before you can address the difficulties in your relationships. Another book I read which is brought up in the marriage 911 course is the book called The Five Love Languages which I'm sure most of you heard. Basically, the basis of this book is that there's five different love languages in the world.

The different types of people that have these types and if you're able to assess these different types in your partner, you should be able to reach their love language and repair your relationship. The Third is a book called The Power by Rhonda Byrne, and it's somewhat religious led, but also has many other historical figures throughout the book.

But if you embrace the principles of The Power, which is basically The Power of Love in the universe and all things. If you do not allow negativity in your life, sure it'll come but if you look at it as a positive that there's always some good coming out of this negative energy. Those negative effects will not stay long in your life, positive thoughts and energies will be attracted to you.

So if you learn to love yourself enough, not to address the negativity in the world. That there's a world and a universe with all positivity that will come your way. Sometimes you may not see it at first or understand it, but it will come. But you must first believe. Believe in your mind, your heart and your soul.

And then the final thing that I did on my own. Is that I started a bucket list. I started writing things down that made myself happy. That she would not allow me to do and that always held me back from things that actually, truly that made me happy. Once I stopped focusing on her, the negativity and things I couldn't control. My heart became full of life, gratitude, ready to turn to the next chapter. To start living again.

So, I wrote down I think in the first 30 minutes, 70 plus items on my bucket list. My number one and number two was to go skydiving and number two was to touch a cloud. I was able to achieve only a couple months after writing down this list. Waiting till summer time to go skydiving with a friend of mine who reached out going thru the same thing, a divorce.

She reached out to me, and for a brief time, we were bucket buddies. She first asked going through this, how I seemed so happy and that's when I let her in on these little secrets. Tara said, "Ok, I'm in, it sounds like fun, I will do your number 1 along with you." I said, "Are you sure?" Because of what I can remember she was petrified of heights. I said, "are you sure?" and she said "Yes!" "Ok, were going skydiving." With her response, an emphatic "Oh, Sh&t!!!" But she's always been a trooper, full of life and ready for the next adventure.

As the day of the jump came, headed to the airfield early in the morning. We had rain earlier that day, and they typically don't let you go up during cloudy overcast but this day they did. And if you're able ever able to do it, even if you're afraid of heights I highly recommended. Adrenaline grabbing things you can do in life. If you have a chance to do them, do it. With this one you feel like a bird you, you feel free and a part of it made me feel closer to my mom up in heaven, up in the clouds.

We all have people in our life, full of life, happy go lucky and excited everyday like a kid. Surround yourself with those people and learn. Learn to live life like a child. Life's too short and filled with unfulfilled dreams. Believe like a child that anything is possible, and be excited, grateful for each new day that we are given. The world is too serious, and thru pains in our life, we slowly lose that part of us as a child. We need the world filled with more of us that overcome these challenges and stay childlike. "Tara, thank you for never losing this outlook on life. Always being you and never changing." "And again, thank you."

Your bucket list though needs to be personal and things that are true to you, that make you happy and that's what makes it so special. I think helps with the healing part of this transition in your life or anything you may be going through. A rough time or patch we may be facing, I think that's why these are all great tools. Because it's personal, it's the real you. And you make the decisions on what works, and what doesn't to change your life.

Listening to motivational speakers, words to boost your confidence and to put your mind in a ready state. Ready to take on the day, to take on a new task or challenge. Studies have shown that in the first 20 minutes of waking up, 15 minutes of positive thoughts and feelings raises serotonin levels. Relieves stress, GH levels and results in an overall better quality of life.

Jim Rohn	Eric Thomas
Tony Robbins	Inky Johnson
Jack Canfield	To name a few
Les Brown	

Another tool is to create a vision board and to surround yourself with quotes, dreams, and wishes that you distinctly have. Now all of our individual goals are different. So, this is a personal quest to take on yourself. That's part of the fun. Keep a notepad on you, write your goals and wishes. Write everything down that touches you throughout the day. As Mr. Rohn has said, "Part of the fun, is crossing them off."

It's the journey; it does not matter how long or how difficult it is to get there. But the goal, is to keep striving and never to give up on your dreams, keep growing. Again, never let someone tell you, you can't do something. If you don't know a skill, learn it or find those to surround yourself to help you achieve this part of your journey.

One thing about life is it may be hard; it may be tough, there's valleys, mountains, twists and turns along the way. But if this life tells you anything, even through the roughest conditions a flower can thrive. It can peer up through concrete, on a rock. It only knows how to be a flower, but there are hardships that it most certainly has to struggle thru to become that flower. But it knows no different other than to become what it was made to be.

You, on the other hand, can be anything you want to be and can achieve anything you want. Keep pushing, never give up. Ask and it shall be given to you, seek and you shall find. Knock and the door will be opened.

"It's not the result that's important; it's who you become in the process of achieving the result." Jack Canfield

"Set a goal so big, that in the process of achieving it. You become someone worth being." Jim Rohn

Helpful Tools:

5-HTTP: Used for calming mood, and Serotonin production. This helps to support emotional well-being and relaxation. Helping to soothe daily stress and tensions. You can get at any vitamin shop or Walmart between 8-20 dollars.

Sinclair Method: If fighting addiction, looking into this. Proven to help fight addiction for over 30yrs and is FDA approved. If you or yourself are struggling, please research.

Drinking days. In and out of darkness but there comes a point in scarcity and fear. You learn "enough, is enough." "I want to stop." "I'm done, I'm finished." "This is not me." "Who I am or want to be." You change and grow. You have been given a blessed life, not to take full advantage of your gifts.

Naltrexone, Vivotrol help break addictions

Motivational Learning: Things that draw interest to you

Vision Boards: To help visualize your dreams every day

Audio Books: Skills to learn to achieve your dreams and happiness

Bucket List: A personal list and life's journey to the things that truly bring you joy and happiness.

Juicing: Fruits and Vegetables, water. To cleanse your body, strengthen your mind and spirit. Make sure to consult a doctor and nutritionist before attempting.

Daily Journal: Keeping a notepad on you for ideas and goals to complete daily. To start building momentum towards your dreams, and the gifts you have been given.

Ch. 16. Waves Crashing a Return 10yrs Later

"Nothing is impossible." "Impossible is an opinion." "How many times has science been proven wrong on what is said to be "The impossible, becomes possible."

—Tony Robbins

Below are words, so kindly gifted from above, sitting in the sand, by the water on the shores of beautiful sunny Florida. Looking out past the sail boats, dancing against the waves, I got this idea to get a balloon and write my mother a message and send it up to her in heaven. Private and one only between us.

These are words I truly believe are gifted from above, so perfect for honoring my mother, in the song I wrote right here at Waterway Park in Merritt Island for her called "I Can't Wait."

"What if heaven had no angels, it had no wings. What if love never died, and all the hurt it brings. When love seems to break and crashes to the ground...you may be in heaven…. but you're all around…..I can see it now…."

As Fate has it 10 years later after losing my mom, I would return taking a job away from family and friends to beautiful sunny Florida. Which I'm not complaining I love it here, the people I have met. New friends, experiences and not to mention the airplane tickets are cheap enough.

Where I can fly home about once a month when I'm feeling lonely or missing my crazy pups.

But the crazy thing is I wasn't supposed to be here; I was supposed to be in Clearwater Florida all the way across the other side of the state. But 5 minutes into my new job they needed help on a project out at Nasa. Being that I had just got into town, no place yet to live and the fact I know nobody here. Being I'm pretty much on my own here I say "yes." I'll take that job on; I'll fix it and save as much money as I can. But what I didn't know was not till the second weekend that I was here. I started to think as I was about heading to the beach, I've been here before. Things looked familiar.

I went to my good friend Gabe's wedding, right here in Cocoa. He married the love of his life, Ashley which he met so many years ago working security at a local bar with me… And that's how they met; he knew from that moment that she was the one. This is the love I've been searching for and he knew when they first met, she's the one.

I drove to Cocoa Beach for their wedding, an amazing time out on the beach in a celebration of two wonderful people finding love in one another. I had never been to a wedding out on the beach before. Sunny with a light breeze off the coast, absolutely gorgeous. Then on the Sunday after, following the wedding getting ready to leave. Preparing for my fourteen-hour drive home that lies ahead of me.

It that was the first Mother's Day without my mom and in 2008. Short story, a lot of us were supposed to fly down, then rent a car and drive back together. But everybody forgot to tell me that they got tickets together and flew round trip. On the other hand, I did not get this information, so I drove from Cincinnati the whole way rocking out to music by myself. Stayed the weekend on the beach at the Hilton. Then shortly after the wedding, I had to drive back alone.

But if this didn't happen, I would not have had this amazing experience. Finding this place, the inspiration for my mom's song and these moments a decade later to share with you now. Getting this wonderful idea to send her personal messages by a balloon. Up in the clouds, a little closer to you mom, up in heaven.

Curves and forks in the road people. Changes in life's plans, they are not often bad, and tend to lead you to where you're ultimately supposed to be, in that moment. And sometimes leads you to the most beautiful places and beautiful surprises.

And being here in Cocoa, away from home, away from family and friends. It is always a little tough but being by the ocean or the water. Seeing certain colors in a sunset or flowers on the side of the road. Especially, that in the color purple or the sight of butterflies always brings me somehow closer to her.

That second weekend I was here I decided to go to Cocoa Beach to check it out and get some sun. Sunday Funday, just to kind of relax, get away for a bit from the work and the stress. But my GPS keeps telling me to go straight down route 1. Not to make a left but my heart and my mind keep telling me to. I kept seeing purple flowers beside the road and that's a signal from my mom, so I took a left to follow the signs.

Follow the signs when you can, take the opportunity when they arise and follow your heart. Let go of control, steady your mind and let life guide you towards your goals and dreams. Believe in yourself, your capabilities and your wishes. Your mind and heart are a powerful tool.

When we are born the heart develops first, showing to be present by day 18. The first traces of the brain do not show up until late into the fourth week of conception. Fears and your thoughts will steer you often times away from your dreams, and as a defense mechanism to keep you away from danger. Have the courage to chase your heart, hopes and dreams.

When your life first started, it started with the heart. Let it lead you as it has when you first were brought to life in your mother's womb.

This is when I ended up driving just past the park, where I wrote her song so many years ago. Sending her a message, the same park where I got this idea, and sent her, her first balloon. I still at this point had no idea but once I looked left after making the turn. More purple flowers along the median, and at a stoplight I see just beyond my view. The original Walmart where I got this idea in the first place.

One I still do for her sending messages every Mother's Day and on her birthday. Letting them go in the wind and for her to receive them up in heaven. Some people may love the idea, some people may think it's corny but it's just something I came up with and I love the idea. I decided to get another balloon, to do the same thing as I've done before, just as fate has made it. The same store, same park a decade earlier, as I've always done. I've always wanted to see something over all these years. I wanted to witness something amazing that would let me know my mom's messages are being received, some kind of sign, anything.

I always send her a balloon on her birthday and on Mother's Day. So, I knew from that point after getting the balloon; I always get a yellow balloon for some reason. Something with butterflies on it for some reason. I'm just drawn to it, and keep in mind with the first balloon and being the first Mother's Day without her.

My grandmother and dad have yet to reveal my mother's notes to us a month later. Where the butterfly connection and the note to my sister Amber hasn't even been shared or revealed. I still keep this tradition, finding a yellow balloon with butterflies and if they have the color purple mixed in. That is always a bonus. But no matter what I always tend to find it, one last balloon with some color yellow in the store. If it has yellow and purple, a butterfly... it's perfect.

The first balloon I saw walking into to this Walmart 10 years ago was a yellow butterfly balloon and I knew that was the one. So, grabbed a sharpie and I wrote my first message to my mom. It's always personal, it's always something to let her know I'm doing okay, family's okay, we miss her, and we love you.

For others that have passed on since then, my grandmother I hope they're all together, up there. And I feel like through this book and experiences they are. And I hope that's what I bring to you all, if nothing else. For those that read these pages and you understand that there's something beyond this life. There is something more powerful than we know or can ever imagine in this universe watching over us all.

God, a higher power, infinite light, something that brings us all together, that there are no coincidences. Everything happens for reason; the timing may not seem right. Hurtful, hateful things that are all are a part of life, but how can we minimize the pain and what are we to learn from this. To make my life or someone else's better from it, these events are made to bring us all together, to make us better it. To capture the all the beauty life has to offer. And when hardships and pain comes, make it short, learn from it and turn the negative into a positive.

And I hope through this; you guys realize that because I know the last six to seven years. I have taken a step back, I've come to realize that this life is what you make it. It's how you perceive things, how you feel every day.

If you wake up with a negative attitude and perception. That is how your day is going to turn out but if you wake up being thankful. Grateful for the people and things in our life. Things will tend to move in the direction of your mind and thoughts. We have a choice to make a life or to design one. I choose the latter, design it the way you want. No one else can do it for you, but have fun with it, chase your dreams.

Whatever it takes to be in a grateful state, one of beauty no matter what happens.

Change your outlook of thinking, find beauty with everything life brings you. It's short. It doesn't mean pain and suffering won't touch our lives. Control your emotions, master them to take on any of life's challenges. Don't stay in pain very long; life is too short. Analyze and you control what you can, nothing's impossible.

Take for instance a sunset or the sunrise, family members that are still around you, that you can call and talk to. The job that you have, the money that you want. Jim Rohn is quoted in saying "You can get more than you got, if you become more than you are." That is so true, write down your dreams, and formulate a plan to receive them. Show that you're serious about the life that you want. If something is keeping you from your dreams, change it.

You can do above and beyond what your current position asks you to do. And it can bring you more money at that position. But I don't like to think of it like that, that money is everything but if it'd what you are truly searching for. It will lead you to where you're supposed to go either in that position or a new one. Or you will create an idea to make the money you deserve. To reach others and help others in this world.

Seek and you shall find. I believe whoever created this life, the universe and the stars wants us to all have our dreams. We all have different dreams that we all can achieve what we want, if we prove without a reasonable doubt that we would do anything to achieve them.

As I return to Merritt Island Waterway Park. After the release of my mom's first balloon. I've always wanted to see something for 10 years, just anything. I always thought I'd see something in the sky. Something amazing, life changing to let me know she's ok. But the thought that there's no planes that fly in this area. There's nothing but clouds and warm sunshine in the blue open air above. What I witnessed was nothing short of a miracle and you can take it how you want. I saw it first in the screen on my phone which I was not going to record at all.

I had out my sister's guitar and was strumming along playing my mom's song that I wrote for her on the shore at this very park so many years earlier. Alone on the first Mother's Day without my mom, leaving my friend's wedding just a few miles down the road. I wanted to honor her in a personal way for myself, my family and anyone who ever came into contact with this amazing woman.

I wrote one of my most heartfelt songs, lyrics that holds a special place in my heart. And I hope for other's that have heard it, that have lost, that it touches them as well. I sat there weeping on the sandy banks, the warm breeze touching my skin. I asked for a blessing, looking up to the skies for the words to honor this special lady.

To let her know how much we all love her, miss her and wish she was still here with us. And with that, with poetry to paper came a blessing. Out of nowhere it filled my heart with poignant words. So perfect and true, to anyone who has ever lost someone, I ask of you to listen. I truly believe most of my writings come from a different part of my heart and soul. Somewhere in a higher thought of thinking and knowing. Somewhere up above.

I've always been able to sense pain, happiness, true feelings thru people. Even those I may never meet, or not truly know. I have always had this gift, and I truly take it as both a blessing. I try to use it to reach those through my feelings, or to relate with what they must be feeling in that moment. As I have my whole life been asked to help others write the songs, they wish they could to honor the one's they love. I think this is my true gift, in healing thru them, and myself on paper.

But as I stood there looking out on the water, getting the balloon from the back seat. Writing a personal message to my mom as I always do.

Something just kept telling me to record it. "Record it, record it." And I guess that's why when you look at my Instagram video posting it starts out about a thousand feet to 1500 feet away from me. Swaying in the wind, back and forth as it dances towards the clouds.

Angel Among Us

Roughly 24 seconds into the video something shocking and miraculous takes place. A warm, glowing beam of light appears from the clouds. Starting just below the clouds flying from left to right. When I first looked at the screen on my phone, I didn't know what it was. As I continue to look thru the screen of my phone in disbelief. I turn to widen my eyes and away from the view of my phone, up into the air above.

I see an Angel in the sky flying softly towards her balloon. White as the purest snow. I feel a connection to the skies and a soft comfort comes over me. Taking notice of what is before me, my eyes focus in and begin to well up. Alone as I once was 10yrs ago, at the same park nestled next to the water. Waiting for a moment, just as this to appear. And now here it is, not knowing whether to cry in happiness, sadness or disbelief. But here is this moment, in all its glory and I'm so grateful to have listened to my heart to share it all with you. "Record it, record it."

I like to believe that it was my mother and I feel in my heart it was. But what I didn't know when I slow down the footage. Pulling it up on a larger screen, pausing frame by frame. Is when it disappears multiple Angels appear in the clouds. It looks to be anywhere from three to five flying above and around the balloon.

Then as they disappear and then the original angel comes back. But quickly looking up to the clouds, I could clearly see an Angel with long brown flowing hair, but you can almost see through it. Still such a different kind of light, so bright, brighter than the sun. A crystal clear

pure white, brighter than anything I had ever seen before...pure. Soothing to the eyes though, shoulders, head, feet, legs and wings flapping. Then it disappeared and then it came back.

C. Stanton

I could not believe my eyes or what I was witnessing, something I have wanted to see for over a decade sending her messages. Something I prayed about and believed in my heart, with everything over the years, that would happen. That the impossible, would appear and become possible. That the mind, heart and soul...our beliefs of ourselves, our dreams, of the universe. I could no longer control my thoughts and emotions as I immediately started to bawl my eyes out.

I called all of my family members and I was kind of scared. Because I've been thankful enough and blessed enough to witness events, where my mom has reached out multiple times after death. To let me and my family know that she is okay, she's not hurting anymore. To send us a message from the heavens above, that you're still around us. I believe people that have moved on they are still around in some sense. We just can't see them but there's little signs that they send, and they give us if we look just hard enough. Guiding us in the right direction and a lot of times we don't believe or want to believe and we don't pay attention to them.

But the last 10 years everything that I have went through. All the pain, the struggles, and I've came out better, stronger from it. I believe she's sensing this to have me help others. Somehow and in some way.

I've always had a huge heart to help people, and that's why I'm taking a negative and turning it into a positive. Going through my divorce, a cancer scare. Just being sick every day, being overworked and losing my dream house. All the materialistic stuff that doesn't even matter anymore, in the greater scheme of things they don't matter.

Angel Among Us

I think that was the bigger picture that I couldn't just rely on positive thinking. I couldn't rely on a book that I read by Rhonda Byrne called the Power to get me through. I couldn't rely on positive motivational speakers. I think I was taught these lessons to try incorporating everything together, to realize that we are all drawn together. There's a reason we're here; there's a reason we're blessed enough to be in this place. To be in this life.

And we all have a purpose, a purpose of each of their own and mine is to write poetry and songs. As well as this book, to show my heart to help people. To give everything that I have to open up to you, to tell this amazing story, to write music that touches you all. And to let you form your own opinions about life.

We look years down the road and recollect troubled times. Times when we feel most alive, good times in our life. And you seem to find out that those trials and tribulations, the good and the bad. Everything that you went through is exactly what you needed. Even if it comes to losing someone close to you, like with me losing my mom. It was hard; it was painful beyond belief. One of the hardest things I've ever experienced. I truly hope nobody ever has to experience what we all went thru as a family. The feeling of the shock, the loss of a parent or loved one with no warning.

But what I did focus on at that moment, was that of my sister. Walking up the street and just screaming. Things weren't registering when it came to her; it wasn't my mom…period. I didn't want to except it, but once she said it the third time. A moment frozen in time, there is no going back. So what next, there is no fixing it or turning back time. But what I focused on was all the good she did do that week. All the things that she talked about for years doing. She completed. All the greatness she completed in her life, being a loving mother.

Then if they would have went on their anniversary. My mom and dad's anniversary vacation with my sisters together. If she would have passed away along the trip or down there in Myrtle Beach. How much harder it would have been on all of us not knowing what happened. Not having her here, in her own bed having to be sent back to Northern Kentucky to be buried.

When you look deep down, you can find even in the worst hurt, grace. And I think at this moment. Looking back through all the tough moments, I was grateful that my dogs were with me, showing me love and gratitude for what I did have. A loving family, loving friends, my niece and little nephews. My mom. They were all with me, in my best of times and the lowest of times. Their love is and has always been with me.

Having not from my mom, striving for us to be better, being the kids, she always saw us to be. Chasing hopes and dreams. Pushing us all towards our individual goals. Never judging and always striving forward, the right way, with no judgement...only that of love.

Laying there with my phone on google to the new testament. Reading passages that related to my relationship with my ex-wife or lack thereof...I believe thru it all, I was at the right place, at the right time. The right people surrounded me at just the right moment....to push me through.

And you should as well, push thru those moments. Push thru the pain. Don't let things and those you cannot control or moments in life take away your dreams. Don't let them die. But yet have them push you towards them, towards those ambitions. Use it for motivation, when they tell you can't, that's impossible. Make it possible and keep fighting till you do, that's how a dream starts. To believe and see in the unseen.

I remember spending the first few days after losing my mom. At night, writing a poem to honor her out under my grandma's carport. At first, it was difficult for my sisters to stay here, so I did to help out with my grandma. Finding solitude out where we shared our last conversation together. The words and memories just flowed to paper, a mother's love. Helping my grandmother with picking out clothes and funeral arrangements with her. It was beyond tough and looking back I'm not quite sure how we all did it. How we made it thru but one thing, we did it together.

I just remember looking thru all these thousands of photos you forced us to take. And as kids we hated it, having to pose all different ways and always taking that one last photo.... then another...then another. Remembering the moment. But in our darkest days, I think we all could not have been more thankful that you put us thru it. Looking back in our time of pain and healing. Mom, you helped us all.

You brought in to perspective, that life is short. It can be taken in an instant. It's often misused, taken for granted and over shadowed. But in those moments, you, even beyond this life brought us happiness, tears, and memories we long forgot. As for myself, other mothers and other families out there. Take the time for the little moments. Capture them when you can through a lens, film or even a pen to paper. Make life timeless and live each moment to its fullest.

C. Stanton

You made me who I am. All of you, my loving family, friends, co workers, people I encounter on the street. Everyday life, a brief smile or short story I ask of, "how did you get here?" "What's your story?" It's all a wonderful journey and we should all be more grateful to have the opportunity we are given each and every day. I'm guilty of it sure, but I'm striving each day to become better at.

You have shaped me into the person I was meant to be, to tell this story. To tell my songs and poetry. To connect and feel what most cannot. I've struggled through hard times and pain, happiness and sorrow. That most seem they are not able to connect with. But I hope in my heart; I can connect with each and every one of you.

Ending…. Every great story starts with a hero, what story do you want to write? What kind of hero do you want to be? What kind of life do you want to live? Sure, there's ups and downs, trials and tribulations. It's just all in how you perceive it, how you take it. How you grow from it, how we move forward. I'm sure we're not all perfect, but in this life, we never stop trying, never stop dreaming, we never stop growing and never stop believing.

So if I can leave you with this. Believe not only in the seen but the unseen. Believe in your heart, believe in your mind, believe in your passions. In your dreams. Never lose sight of them, remain child-like. Never let your dreams grow tired or old. Our bodies and our minds may, but always follow them and your unwavering heart. From the light of day into the darkening of the night. The human spirit is an amazing thing. Even through hardships, it has an amazing ability to overcome overwhelming odds. Reach the hearts and minds of others, seamlessly thousands of miles away. To show love in extraordinary moments of compassion, in great times of pain. Crossing this life to the next, to show us signs that we are all here for a purpose, a reason. That love conquers all things, and even through death can still show its way.

I leave you with this, leaving my heart out to these pages. Some may believe, some may not. But leave an open mind…. that Angels do live Amongst us.

C. Stanton

Ch. 17. A Book Finished...or So I Thought

And so, I thought I had the book finished. The final chapter but an amazing 2 weeks that I've come home being around family and friends. The core group, the ones that started this whole big journey of writing and singing. Seeing family and friends talking about life, telling stories. And what I didn't know is that the idea I had for my music video for walk in my footsteps, wasn't the idea that was planned.

And I always felt like my songs were from a higher place. The words were given to me from a higher place, using me as a messenger. One of my favorite bible verses Matthew 7:7 ask and it shall be given to you, seek, and ye shall find, knock and it shall be opened unto you.

And what I did was I asked for an unbelievable goal to help find a Farm property to be able to film the idea for walk in my footsteps, my first music video. And a journey over the next 3 days that would lead me to a beautiful farm in the southwest sky. I could not have planned it better myself. To a gorgeous farm at 6 in the morning on a Wednesday.

With all the amazing, blessed things that have occurred in my life. Blessed cannot even describe how I feel towards my life, family and friends. And how we're all connected thru every encounter, every person these last couple of weeks since being home has been nothing but a reminder of that. And how small the world really is when we actually choose to listen and take notice small little details that leads us where our life is supposed to go.

When you let go of all control and let the higher power, infinite light, God whatever you believe lead you with your heart where you're supposed to go. Your purpose. And I've been searching for a farm to film the music video for 4-6 months back home not able to find one, but I had a star that just seems a little bit brighter Wednesday morning. That led me towards Big Bone Lick State Park but as I got to the turn to make a right. The star was to the left and it was telling me from the night before. My experience to follow it to it disappears behind the trees, so I did that morning.

When I stopped, I found the most perfect farm with a serene sky and everything that I wanted. An older Farmhouse, a barn and gorgeous landscape. Then from leading that way to the street, I've never been down in my whole life. Which actually led me out to my best friend Brian's old house and he was the one with his family that first got me to get up on stage and take a chance at singing. One night when I was 21-22 years old, going 3 weekends in a row that they got me in there and listening to other singers. To getting up on stage, singing Don't Take the Girl by Tim McGraw.

Because they knew I knew every Tim McGraw song on the planet. And then from this, led into town to pay homage to my hometown of Florence Kentucky where everything started. My hometown ice cream shop Fillmore's, which has the best banana shake on the planet. They are kind enough to want to put my name and album up on their Banner. And then from this, it let me back out to my mom's Cemetery location where things that happened let me to another part of the story. That I didn't even know existed that the higher power, ultimate light whatever you believe. God took me on another unbelievable journey.

That led me to these two little girl's cemetery plot locations that everything about butterflies, the golden dragonfly, messages from another place that follow me around Angels Among Us. This whole book, the whole purpose of it was how interconnected we are as a human species. And then also that there's Angels Among Us every day that if we take notice, people that don't take credit for little things that they do to brighten someone's day.

But it let me to two little girls' gravestones which I want to contact through Facebook privately to let them know the story if they wish. But my grandmother when I was a kid always said that I would come out and spend time at a cemetery, to do service. And God would give me the answers that I was searching for, thru messages.

And everything that I was talking about actual personal messages on headstones out there with my key signs. The color purple, butterflies kept leading me sporadically for 7 & a half hours to give me the messages that I needed. That my songs aren't actually mine, but from him. Only he can write these songs and lyrics. And I'm so thankful for that and that's another reason why I'm pretty much just giving this book away to help others.

While I'm giving my music away because it's not mine. It's his, it's ultimately his. How following your heart, walking in faith led to a message out on a tree that I did not carve. That I will share in the book thru pictures but I'm trying to be respectful to the people and there families out of this cemetery. As I do not want anything to be damaged or anything to come of it other than that of love and goodness.

But every question I had having signals and messages sent to me over and over and over again led me to this tree. One I never took notice, one I did not carve, and I'm just going to include it on these final pages. For others to take as it is, and believe what they wish to believe.

Along with my video of the Angel in the sky out of Merritt island waterway park. That for 10 years sending messages to heaven to my mom by balloon. Always believing I would capture something. One that kept saying to record, record. I've seen in the sky that started this whole book, telling the story about my mom as she's reached at the other people even after death. That there's something bigger than than ourselves in this life. That everyday we walk among angels, that life is a full circle, surrounded in love, how we're all connected. A lot of times we don't notice them. We don't notice a little thing, little miracles in our life every day that someone else gives to us. From this book, I hope you take things slow, a little extra notice. We often don't take notice of how connected we truly are.

Here's one final story that I've totally forgotten about, till I visited my friend Donald back home in Kentucky. My first CD that I released I did some local shows at a place called Media Play that's no longer around and met a family from Toronto. There was about 15 of them that was going on a trip to Florida. The older grandmother around 95 years old came up to me and wanted me to sign a bunch of CDs that they bought. I talked to them for a little while about there trip and family traditions. Telling me that they always get CDs and listen to them together on the way to Florida from Toronto is a family.

Angel Among Us

3 to 4 years later I'm in Clearwater Florida down at Madeira Beach and I'm singing karaoke at a local bar. When a 95-year old lady comes up to me and tugs on my shirt and ask if I'm the same Clint Stanton from Florence Kentucky that sings. And I said possibly and that's when she pulls out my old CD from years prior that they bought and still listen to this day in front of 15 to 20 of my coworkers.

This past year when I'm in Cocoa Beach working on the other side of Florida. Two and a half hours from Madeira Beach I'm telling a friend of mine, a coworker that story that for some reason popped in my head at this perfect moment. As I'm telling the story, a blonde headed lady next to me tapped me on the shoulder and says the family from Toronto "that you were just talking about." I said "yes." They actually talks about you a lot and they are my next door neighbor's."

When I was two and a half hours away from that location in a random small bar telling a friend of mine at the exact time that she was there. She had never been there before but had to come there for work. She heard about this place called Dogs in Titusville Florida for good food and good and cheap drinks.

And I haven't thought of this story in years, and for some reason that day I was talking to my buddy about it how we're all connected. How small life really is when we look at it. Every relationship, every chance meeting really isn't by chance. And she had never been there before. And she just happened to be their next-door neighbors and got in touch with them through Facebook being able to reach out to them.

So, when you think of things, chance meetings are they really? Its every friendship, every chance meeting, every relationship really is meant to lead you to where you're supposed to go and towards your purpose.

To notice and thank those in their life that show them love, making them happy. That, that makes us happy and I hope nothing else from this book. That I was able to help just one person through these pages. That was my whole goal in writing this, is just to help one person make their life a little bit easier, little bit better then there are Angels Among Us. If we truly look at each and every day as a little miracles in our life. How we're all interconnected that there are Angels Among Us each and every day.

Love is everything you ever wanted to be. It is us, it is you it is me. Its every dream you ever had or thought about having. It is God, the ultimate. The alpha and omega. The beginning, the end. The in between. He is all of us, and we are of him. 6 degrees of separation, I believe it's actually 7. God being the center of all things, but we are not separated at all. In fact, thru his love and our own we are all truly perfectly connected.

How quick we are to point at good. We should take a deep breath and think that of what we cannot foresee. That life is full circle, surrounded in love and faith. Believing in something within your heart, something unseen.

Lead first with your heart, get your mind and thoughts out of the way for a second. Then lean even deeper with your soul. Your connection with God. Then with your decision making and believe. Put him first, even in the most difficult situations and let him take the lead. Let her take the lead for once and find your ultimate joy and peace. They have done so much for us, to be here on earth. We should take notice, give praise to God and all of our graces.

Angel Among Us

God is love, full circle, both mother and father. All things as we know it. With a most perfect gift for each of us every day. To walk out in nature, the trees, to the air we breathe. Those we pass by every day at the convenient store or on the street. Keep your guard up and pay close attention. If its Gods will, and that of ours being free will of your own. As God gives you both love and the will to make your own choices from your heart and soul. Follow and God will lead you on your own personal, amazing journey towards your own purpose. That it's true, Angels are truly Among Us.

"Walk In my Footsteps"

Written by: Clint Stanton
Performed by: Clint Stanton

Walk in my footsteps little boy.
See the whole world thru my eyes.
A promise to you, to always treat you good.
Always want to be in your life.

But things change, no matter what you do.
Always know in your heart, I wanted you.
But it never works out, no matter how you plan.
Walk in my footsteps little boy and be my little man.

I know you there may be many questions.
On why you felt, I left.
I know I may not seem to have the answers.
To all the brokenness your dealt.
But as long as you trust in your heart.
For a love, I so greatly show.
You'll find the answers you seek.
In your heart later down the road.

But things change, no matter what you do.
Always know in your heart, I wanted you.
But it never works out, no matter how you plan.
Walk in my footsteps little boy and be my little man.

No matter how you push me away.
I'll always be there for you.

When you stubble and can't carry on.
That's where my guiding light shines thru.
I never give up on a child.
No matter how far they stray.
Although, I'm up here in heaven.
In my heart by your side, I'll stay.

But things change, no matter what you do.
Always know in your heart, I wanted you.
But it never works out, no matter how you plan.
Walk in my footsteps little boy,
Walk in my footsteps little boy and be my little man.

Author Bio:

"Never let someone's opinion of you, shape your reality…"

Clint Stanton grew up in the small town of Florence, Kentucky. He attended Northern Kentucky University before going on to work in the IT industry for the next 20 years and is also a gifted songwriter and poet. He currently lives in Nashville, Tennessee with his 3 dogs, Roo, Charlie and Moose.

Now his first book, **Angels Among Us,** is completed and ready to be published. It is the true story of how the trauma and loss from a divorce brought about an amazing self-learning experience that he had never expected, through his mother reaching out to her after death.

In his spare time, Clint has a wide range of interests which include singing and writing country music, writing poetry and enjoying all different kinds of movies. Which he is currently writing a movie comedy script with his childhood friend Brian. He also enjoys spending time by the ocean and hanging out with family and friends as often as he can.

As far as the future goes, Clint hopes to continue writing music and singing songs that touch others for as long as he can. He is methodically working his way through a long and extensive bucket list, with sky diving being at the top of the pile. He doesn't exclude anything in his list and is always open to new ideas and suggestions.

He would also like to write more books, with a children's one on his list of next ambitious targets.

You can contact Clint Stanton, follow him, or see what he is writing at:

Website - www.clintstanton.com

Twitter - twitter@theclintstanton

Facebook -   @theclintstanton,

@clintstantonmusic,

@clint.stanton.94

YouTube – Clint Stanton

Instagram – theclintstanton

Email - AngelsAmongUsbook@gmail.com

Manager – Chris Keaton chris@chriskeaton.com

Music available online

Feel free to leave a book review at Amazon and Kindle

Reader's guide:

I created this book out of love and for you the reader to enjoy it anyway possible. Any way that you wish to read it from chapter 1 the very first beginning, the acknowledgement page, from the end to the middle. Any way you wish. It was meant for you and you can enjoy it any way that you wish.

Basically, you can use the index pages to find things that may you may be dealing with. Your personal self, troubles or wanting to improve upon. Something that catches your eye and is relatable to you. Maybe it's addiction, maybe it's the loss of a loved one, maybe it's needing motivation going through a tough relationship or marriage. I wrote this book out of love to help people anyway I can. Taking my time and leaning on my heart with each page you hold in your hand for you. And I think all my trials and tribulations everything that I've ever went through there's a reason for it.

Because how else am I going to write a book to help people through things, if I haven't lived it myself. How's it going to be relatable to you, the reader and I hope you truly do read this book. That you enjoy it and I hope to at least help one person. Then, this book to me is a success. To change your perspective on life, what's truly possible and if you learn one thing from it to help you become quite possibly just a little bit of a better person. You matter to me, and your dreams matter.

I hope to make life thru these pages, a little bit sweeter for you and your loved ones. For you to chase your dreams, for you to find the love of your life and create the life that you've always wanted and deserve. I hope through these pages I give you at least one notion or at least one idea that you can use to capture your dreams. Because ultimately that's why I wrote the book.

My love for people and all things. To help to realize that through your toughest trials and tribulations you can create the life that you want. With that enjoy the book, you learn to love yourself a little more, love others and chase your dreams; not letting anything stop you from your goals and purpose.

I wrote with his ultimate help, words of love. That if God see's fit, it will reach your heart and draw you closer to him and the bible. Enjoy and leave me a review. Thank you and in his name.

Amen.

Index:

5-HTTP, 170
Abraham Lincoln, iii, 25, 135
accident, 38, 153, 155, 156, 158
Accident is the Mother of Invention, 147
Accidents is the mother of invention, 155
acknowledge, iii, 100
Acknowledgments, iii
addiction, 84, 170, 198
adversity, 115, 157, 161, 162
afterlife, 1, 2, 31
Air Force, 34, 46
Always, v, vi, 3, 14, 75, 158, 161, 168, 190, 194, 195
always dream, iv
amazing, iii, iv, v, vi, vii, viii, 1, 2, 6, 12, 15, 17, 18, 20, 29, 30, 34, 36, 41, 42, 46, 47, 52, 54, 56, 61, 64, 69, 78, 83, 87, 88, 89, 97, 99, 104, 105, 108, 112, 113, 118, 119, 137, 143, 145, 155, 164, 172, 173, 174, 177, 181, 184, 187, 193, 196
Amazing, vi, 11, 85
ambulance, 53, 54, 138
Amish, 100
angel, ii, x, 55, 71, 179
Angel, xii, 179, 190
angels, x, xi, 6, 171, 190
Angels Among Us, i, xiii, 189, 192, 196
Angels are Among Us, iii, iv
Anonymous, 9, 67, 99, 165
Arkansas, 106
Arnold mode, 149
ashamed, 4, 121, 130, 165
Assuring, 91
Audio Books, 170
author, 151, 154
Baby Boy, ii
balloon, 171, 173, 174, 175, 177, 178, 179, 190
beautiful, vi, vii, x, 2, 14, 15, 18, 28, 30, 31, 37,

46, 47, 61, 63, 64, 67, 71, 73, 74, 88, 91, 92, 96, 100, 104, 106, 110, 121, 123, 135, 147, 148, 157, 160, 171, 173, 187
beauty of nature, 95
become a better person, xi, 130
beliefs, 29, 31, 39, 41, 89, 96, 119, 180
believe, iii, xii, 2, 3, 5, 7, 13, 18, 20, 21, 23, 26, 27, 28, 29, 30, 31, 38, 41, 50, 55, 59, 65, 80, 81, 85, 86, 87, 89, 90, 97, 99, 101, 108, 119, 124, 126, 131, 132, 139, 142, 151, 152, 153, 155, 156, 158, 159, 164, 166, 171, 177, 178, 179, 180, 182, 183, 184, 185, 188, 192
Believe, iii, 20, 23, 27, 89, 141, 166, 168, 174, 184
believe in the unseen, 7, 97
believing in love, vii
Ben Franklin, 17
Bennie Hill, 36
Bible, 31, 123, 129, 166
Big Bone Lick State Park, 188

Billboard Country charts, 14
blessed, iii, iv, ix, xi, 11, 18, 43, 137, 143, 170, 180, 181, 187
blessing, iv, viii, 10, 18, 155, 178
blue eyes, vi, 105
blueprint, 119
bond, 36, 37, 127
brokenness, 194
brother, v, 35, 50, 52, 55, 63, 93, 109, 112, 143, 144
brothers, vi, vii, 3, 6, 11, 12, 42, 51, 53, 60, 64, 72, 133, 138, 139, 144, 164
Brothers, 78
bucket list, 86, 118, 130, 131, 143, 167, 168, 196
butterflies, 19, 43, 65, 139, 173, 175, 189
butterfly, 65, 155, 175
cabin, 83, 85, 87, 90, 91, 93, 94, 101, 103, 104, 106, 107, 109, 110, 125, 132
Cambridge University, 29
cancer, 35, 46, 47, 121, 180
challenge yourself, 157

challenging, vi, 18, 127, 142, 163
chance, xiii, 3, 6, 13, 15, 25, 34, 41, 69, 78, 108, 110, 131, 135, 145, 153, 167, 188, 191
change, ix, 10, 11, 12, 19, 21, 25, 27, 28, 29, 34, 39, 52, 80, 83, 85, 89, 117, 119, 123, 124, 133, 160, 168, 170, 177, 194, 195, 198
Charles R. Swindoll, 33
Chase, 22, 23, 25
Chase your dreams, 22
chasing, ix, 3, 19, 22, 28, 37, 42, 73, 74, 133, 157
children, 2, 18, 33, 65, 133, 154, 197
Christian, 61, 129, 165
Christianity, 1
Christmas, 3, 11, 19, 40, 60, 78, 101, 126, 133
Cincinnati, 9, 33, 55, 61, 67, 72, 74, 109, 133, 140, 143, 172
clear, 37, 62, 83, 86, 92, 144, 179
Clearwater Florida, 172, 191
Clint, viii, xiii, 6, 10, 86, 101, 136, 137, 191, 194, 196, 197
clouds, 7, 92, 144, 145, 147, 168, 173, 177, 178, 179
Cocoa Beach, 164, 172, 173, 191
coincidences, 5, 175
commitment, 71, 117, 131, 151, 152, 153
commitments, 153
complete, 56, 107, 170
confused, 74, 100, 106, 116, 149
connection, 6, 52, 109, 175, 179, 192
control, xi, 30, 48, 49, 79, 118, 123, 124, 130, 131, 133, 142, 153, 159, 162, 163, 167, 173, 176, 180, 182, 188
dad, iv, v, vii, viii, ix, 2, 3, 4, 10, 11, 13, 25, 33, 41, 42, 46, 51, 52, 53, 54, 62, 63, 65, 67, 68, 70, 71, 78, 102, 103, 104, 109, 110, 111, 125, 132, 133, 139, 140, 148, 154, 155, 175, 182
Dad, iv, 3, 9, 55, 103, 122
Daily Journal, 170
decision, vii, 6, 95, 119, 192

decisions, x, 6, 21, 34, 74, 118, 142, 168
Deepak Chopra, 147
Depression, 121
desires, 27, 29, 39
different, xi, 5, 6, 25, 26, 28, 41, 46, 59, 61, 69, 77, 78, 80, 81, 93, 94, 109, 110, 115, 116, 124, 126, 127, 131, 132, 145, 153, 155, 156, 157, 158, 164, 166, 169, 177, 178, 179, 183, 196
divorced, 108
Donato's, 45, 136, 137, 143
don't do nothing stupid, 122
Don't Take the Girl, viii, 188
Dr. Masaru Emoto, 118, 127
dream, iii, viii, 2, 5, 13, 18, 21, 23, 26, 27, 28, 33, 35, 40, 52, 57, 60, 62, 73, 86, 87, 88, 89, 93, 94, 99, 101, 102, 104, 107, 108, 110, 116, 120, 125, 132, 133, 135, 151, 153, 157, 159, 180, 183, 192
dreamed, 33, 70, 77, 87, 93, 117, 128, 132, 159

dreamer, 9, 14, 20, 25, 107, 133
dreaming, 14, 15, 57, 86, 101, 184
dreams, iii, iv, vii, viii, ix, x, xi, 3, 9, 13, 14, 17, 18, 19, 20, 21, 22, 23, 25, 26, 27, 28, 29, 30, 34, 35, 36, 37, 40, 42, 43, 52, 59, 63, 64, 69, 70, 73, 74, 81, 84, 85, 86, 87, 89, 93, 96, 101, 107, 116, 119, 126, 133, 141, 142, 151, 152, 156, 157, 158, 159, 160, 161, 162, 163, 165, 168, 169, 170, 174, 176, 177, 180, 182, 184, 198, 199
E equals events, 163
E equals R equals O, 163
Edison Elementary, x, 19
Eleanor Roosevelt, 59
embarrassed, 4, 130
embrace, 71, 121, 166
Eric Thomas, 115, 118, 168
experience, 2, 29, 41, 64, 88, 118, 125, 145, 173, 181, 188, 196
experiences, 31, 43, 64, 65, 69, 124, 158, 161, 171, 175
Facebook, 189, 191, 197

faith, vii, x, 23, 89, 97, 112, 158, 164, 189, 192
family, iii, iv, v, viii, ix, x, xiii, 1, 4, 5, 11, 13, 20, 21, 25, 26, 28, 33, 34, 35, 38, 40, 41, 42, 43, 46, 47, 50, 51, 52, 54, 55, 56, 60, 62, 63, 65, 72, 73, 74, 78, 79, 80, 81, 83, 84, 85, 107, 109, 110, 111, 112, 113, 115, 116, 119, 120, 121, 123, 125, 127, 129, 133, 135, 138, 139, 154, 158, 159, 163, 171, 173, 175, 176, 177, 180, 181, 182, 184, 187, 190, 191, 196
Fat, Sick and Nearly Dead, 82
father, 14, 39, 54, 72, 111, 113, 193
Fear is False Evidence Appearing Real, 89
Finding a Dream, 99
flower, 10, 92, 110, 139, 169
flowers, 31, 43, 97, 173, 174
focus, 29, 30, 35, 54, 55, 73, 83, 118, 121, 125, 129, 130, 179, 181
Focus, 27, 30

follow, iv, x, xi, 10, 27, 68, 91, 93, 96, 102, 103, 136, 173, 184, 188, 197
follow our hearts, xi
foolish, 6
foresee, 21, 192
forever grateful, iv
Forrest Gump, 35, 36, 43, 93
friend, ii, vii, viii, 1, 2, 12, 26, 28, 35, 43, 52, 59, 67, 70, 73, 76, 104, 113, 122, 144, 151, 154, 167, 172, 177, 188, 190, 191, 196
friends, iii, x, xiii, 1, 2, 4, 5, 11, 13, 21, 31, 34, 60, 73, 81, 83, 107, 111, 112, 113, 115, 116, 117, 119, 120, 123, 125, 127, 135, 158, 159, 163, 171, 173, 182, 184, 187, 196
gathered, 55, 56, 71, 138
goal, 2, 29, 30, 37, 86, 169, 187, 192
God, iii, ix, 1, 14, 23, 39, 49, 55, 81, 107, 119, 124, 127, 156, 162, 175, 188, 189, 192, 193, 199
God., iii, ix, 192

gorgeous, 42, 68, 87, 94, 172, 187
Grammy Award for Best Male Country Vocal Performance, 14
grandma, iv, viii, 4, 7, 46, 48, 51, 53, 54, 108, 135, 136, 140, 143, 150, 183
Grandma, viii, 51, 52, 108, 136, 137, 138, 151
grandmother, 11, 15, 36, 38, 40, 41, 46, 47, 48, 49, 50, 53, 54, 60, 61, 62, 64, 65, 92, 107, 108, 111, 132, 133, 143, 150, 155, 158, 159, 164, 175, 183, 189, 190
grandpaw, v, 7
greatest laugh, vi
growing, vi, 11, 33, 34, 39, 40, 140, 169, 184
guide, 6, 155, 173, 198
guiding light, 195
happiness, 29, 31, 57, 83, 116, 130, 136, 138, 142, 163, 170, 178, 179, 183, 184
hardships, 4, 9, 12, 20, 21, 28, 37, 45, 114, 158, 159, 163, 169, 176, 184

healing, 12, 168, 178, 183
heart, iii, v, vi, vii, viii, x, xi, xii, 1, 2, 4, 5, 6, 9, 10, 12, 14, 15, 18, 19, 20, 21, 23, 25, 26, 28, 30, 31, 35, 37, 38, 39, 41, 42, 43, 49, 52, 57, 63, 65, 68, 69, 70, 80, 81, 87, 88, 89, 91, 92, 94, 96, 99, 101, 102, 107, 108, 111, 117, 121, 122, 123, 127, 130, 131, 139, 142, 143, 151, 155, 156, 157, 158, 159, 161, 162, 164, 166, 167, 173, 174, 178, 179, 180, 181, 184, 185, 188, 192, 194, 195, 198, 199
heartbroken, 4
hearts, vii, 43, 56, 69, 94, 119, 133, 184
heaven, 31, 43, 89, 96, 104, 107, 126, 137, 168, 171, 173, 174, 190, 195
Heaven, 37, 89, 97
Heaven on Earth, 89
help, 1, 4, 6, 13, 15, 19, 23, 29, 31, 34, 35, 39, 41, 42, 46, 49, 56, 68, 73, 74, 75, 77, 78, 79, 80, 84, 86, 90, 107,

111, 116, 119, 120, 121, 129, 131, 138, 148, 150, 163, 165, 169, 170, 172, 177, 178, 180, 181, 183, 187, 192, 198, 199
Helpful Tools, 170
helping, v, 1, 18, 34, 42, 77, 106, 125
Henry Youngman, 33
honest, 26
hope, iii, iv, v, vii, x, xiii, 4, 6, 11, 18, 25, 43, 51, 69, 113, 115, 120, 125, 130, 156, 158, 163, 175, 176, 178, 181, 184, 190, 192, 198
How connected life, xii
how connected we truly are, 190
idea, x, 9, 40, 61, 70, 77, 80, 102, 130, 132, 143, 159, 171, 173, 174, 177, 187, 199
impactful, 34
influences, 151
Inky Johnson, 168
interconnected, xi, 189, 192
Jack Canfield, 118, 163, 168, 169
Jenny, 36, 37, 38, 39
Jesus Christ, iii

Jim Rohn, iii, xi, 17, 21, 22, 24, 29, 45, 118, 160, 165, 168, 169, 176
Jim Valvano, 18
Joe Cross, 82
John Calipari, 141
John Wooden, 1
Jonathan Swift, 59
journey, iii, x, 11, 14, 18, 20, 26, 80, 89, 96, 116, 124, 132, 149, 153, 156, 161, 169, 170, 184, 187, 193
juicing, 82, 83, 84
Juicing, 170
Kentucky, iv, 9, 33, 34, 49, 61, 76, 77, 87, 88, 90, 91, 95, 99, 103, 108, 120, 125, 129, 140, 141, 182, 188, 190, 191, 196
King Arthur, 36
laughter, viii, ix, xiii, 10, 12, 19, 35, 62, 78, 138
learn, 2, 4, 5, 6, 13, 15, 22, 26, 28, 29, 41, 42, 81, 82, 111, 117, 118, 119, 121, 123, 124, 127, 128, 130, 131, 141, 142, 157, 158, 160, 161, 163, 164, 166, 168, 169, 170, 176, 198, 199

learned, 6, 9, 26, 79, 115, 127, 131, 142, 161, 165
legacy, v, 43
Les Brown, 23, 24, 118, 168
Lessons to Live by, 165
life, iv, v, vi, vii, viii, ix, x, xi, xiii, 1, 2, 3, 4, 5, 6, 10, 11, 13, 14, 15, 17, 18, 19, 20, 21, 22, 23, 24, 25, 26, 27, 28, 29, 30, 31, 34, 35, 36, 37, 39, 40, 42, 43, 45, 47, 48, 49, 50, 51, 53, 54, 57, 59, 60, 61, 62, 63, 65, 68, 69, 71, 72, 73, 74, 76, 77, 78, 79, 80, 81, 82, 83, 84, 85, 86, 87, 89, 93, 94, 96, 101, 111, 114, 117, 118, 119, 120, 121, 122, 123, 124, 126, 127, 131, 135, 137, 138, 139, 141, 142, 143, 145, 147, 149, 150, 151, 152, 153, 155, 156, 157, 158, 159, 160, 161, 162, 163, 164, 165, 166, 167, 168, 169, 170, 172, 173, 174, 175, 176, 177, 178, 181, 182, 183, 184, 185, 187, 190, 191, 192, 194, 198, 199
Life, iv, vii, xi, 6, 13, 20, 22, 23, 26, 28, 29, 31, 33, 39, 40, 49, 69, 71, 85, 115, 142, 156, 168
life time, 18
life's little detours, 161
lifting the world up, xii
list of goals, 22
Logan's restaurant, 104, 108, 113
lose my voice, 153
Losing a mother, 7
Loss, 2, 9
lost soul, 6
Louisville, 19, 76, 108, 120
love, ii, iii, iv, v, vii, ix, x, xi, xii, 1, 2, 4, 5, 6, 7, 9, 11, 12, 13, 15, 18, 20, 22, 23, 25, 26, 27, 28, 34, 37, 41, 42, 43, 49, 52, 67, 69, 71, 73, 76, 79, 84, 85, 88, 89, 107, 110, 111, 112, 115, 116, 117, 118, 119, 120, 121, 122, 123, 124, 125, 126, 127, 129, 130, 131, 132, 133, 139, 141, 142, 145, 156, 158, 160, 162, 163, 164, 166, 171, 172, 174, 175, 178, 182, 183, 184,

189, 190, 192, 193, 194, 198, 199
Love, ii, iv, 1, 2, 4, 14, 20, 25, 107, 117, 160, 166, 192
Lynyrd Skynyrd, 154
Madeira Beach, 191
Mamaw, iv
manage, 77
marriage, 5, 69, 71, 75, 117, 129, 130, 131, 132, 165, 166, 198
married, 34, 55, 63, 67, 68, 70, 71, 73, 116, 127, 128, 172
Matthew 7:7, 187
meant to be, 5, 45, 46, 78, 123, 127, 142, 184
memories, x, 11, 35, 38, 42, 43, 47, 48, 51, 56, 61, 73, 94, 133, 135, 139, 143, 150, 183
mental challenges, 56
mentally, 35, 75, 80
mind, v, viii, xi, xii, 4, 9, 12, 15, 19, 20, 21, 22, 23, 25, 30, 43, 45, 50, 51, 52, 56, 69, 75, 82, 87, 91, 92, 95, 96, 105, 116, 119, 128, 139, 142, 144, 148, 156, 159, 160, 161, 162, 166, 168, 170, 173, 175, 176, 180, 184, 185, 192

miracle, 18, 28, 96, 177
mom, ii, iv, v, vi, vii, viii, 1, 2, 4, 6, 7, 9, 10, 11, 13, 14, 15, 18, 20, 25, 33, 35, 37, 38, 40, 42, 43, 45, 46, 47, 48, 49, 50, 51, 52, 53, 55, 57, 59, 60, 61, 62, 63, 64, 65, 67, 72, 78, 86, 87, 88, 92, 94, 96, 97, 101, 102, 104, 105, 107, 108, 109, 110, 111, 112, 113, 114, 119, 123, 124, 125, 126, 133, 136, 137, 138, 145, 150, 154, 155, 156, 159, 164, 168, 171, 172, 173, 174, 175, 177, 178, 180, 181, 182, 183, 188, 190
Mom, iv, 9, 13, 38, 47, 48, 49, 56, 107, 138, 183
moment, vii, x, xi, 4, 5, 7, 10, 12, 14, 20, 21, 23, 25, 26, 29, 30, 35, 37, 39, 45, 47, 48, 50, 52, 55, 64, 67, 69, 70, 71, 73, 74, 76, 81, 84, 93, 96, 102, 108, 110, 111, 120, 122, 123, 125, 126, 127, 129, 138, 139, 144, 147, 148, 149, 150, 151,

154, 157, 162, 172, 173, 178, 179, 181, 182, 183, 191
moments, v, vi, vii, xi, 2, 5, 6, 10, 20, 31, 39, 47, 48, 53, 62, 69, 70, 74, 84, 121, 126, 127, 130, 137, 139, 142, 143, 173, 182, 183, 184
Moments, 39, 53
momentum, 23, 83, 130, 162, 170
money, 18, 29, 35, 41, 45, 52, 74, 76, 78, 84, 112, 116, 129, 132, 133, 152, 153, 158, 159, 172, 176, 177
Monty Python, 36
Mother Teresa, 89
Mother's Day, 10, 36, 172, 174, 175, 177
Motivational Learning, 170
Ms. Roger's, x, 19, 20
munchkin, 40, 54, 60, 62, 80
music, viii, x, xiii, 10, 11, 13, 38, 45, 76, 121, 153, 158, 159, 173, 181, 187, 196
Myrtle Beach, 46, 47, 48, 125, 182
Naltrexone, 170

Nashville, xiii, 9, 13, 15, 35, 45, 67, 68, 72, 107, 196
nature, 31, 40, 105, 131, 155, 161, 193
need, vii, 4, 6, 15, 22, 23, 28, 30, 47, 49, 79, 85, 88, 89, 93, 112, 115, 118, 120, 121, 124, 125, 129, 131, 137, 149, 153, 156, 157, 159, 161, 163, 168
negative thoughts, 81, 86, 119, 162
negativity, 17, 83, 128, 160, 166, 167
Netflix, 45, 82
never in a million years, 99
new outlook, 81
no doubt, 60, 69, 94
O equals outcome, 163
opportunities, 52, 85, 160, 163
opportunity, 23, 36, 76, 78, 158, 161, 173, 184
opposite, 29
pain, 1, 4, 5, 6, 11, 13, 21, 30, 31, 35, 39, 41, 46, 49, 50, 52, 55, 56, 57, 63, 75, 76, 77, 80, 82, 83, 111, 119, 120, 121, 125, 127, 138, 139, 142, 147, 148, 149, 150, 152, 153,

156, 162, 176, 178, 180, 182, 183, 184
painful, 51, 181
panoramic, 92, 100
panoramic view, 92
papaw, v
paper, 1, 9, 12, 26, 27, 51, 54, 64, 65, 99, 155, 159, 178, 183
paradise, 34
passionate, 9, 13, 41, 86, 165
pastor, 71, 112
peaceful, 34, 40, 47, 54, 75, 94, 147
peacefully, 57
perception, 27, 176
perspective, 5, 11, 153, 156, 157, 158, 159, 161, 163, 183, 198
physically, 75, 138, 141, 149
pictures, 5, 46, 47, 48, 54, 72, 87, 88, 99, 101, 102, 103, 109, 111, 120, 189
poem, 12, 183
poetry, 9, 12, 42, 121, 178, 181, 184, 196
police, 92, 150
positive outlook, 81, 87, 137
Positive thinking, 17
Positive Thinking, 17
Power, 23, 26, 80, 81, 83, 166, 181
property, ix, 41, 42, 83, 85, 87, 88, 91, 92, 93, 94, 96, 100, 101, 102, 103, 104, 105, 106, 107, 108, 109, 110, 112, 113, 115, 187
Proverbs 23:7, 19
purple, 43, 60, 61, 92, 110, 173, 174, 175, 189
purpose, ii, iii, xi, xii, 1, 2, 4, 5, 12, 23, 26, 43, 80, 121, 124, 147, 158, 163, 181, 185, 188, 192, 193, 199
R equals response, 163
reality, xii, 17, 18, 24, 87, 119, 126, 132, 159, 196
redbud trees, 85, 87, 91, 92, 94, 95, 104, 110
redbuds, 101
reincarnated, 2, 31
relationship, ix, xi, xiii, 29, 116, 126, 129, 130, 160, 166, 182, 191, 192, 198
relationships, 31, 129, 132, 166
retired, 49, 109
Rhonda Byrne, 80, 166, 181

right direction, 85, 91, 92, 180
Rupp, 143, 144, 150
sacrifice, 21
saddened, 4
sadness, xi, 26, 56, 129, 138, 179
Schwarzenegger, 148, 151
seek, 1, 2, 4, 13, 28, 123, 124, 169, 187, 194
serotonin, 83, 168
shall, 1, 4, 123, 169, 177, 187
significant, 19, 64, 84
signs, x, 43, 93, 94, 96, 108, 110, 111, 116, 159, 173, 180, 185, 189
Sinclair Method, 170
singer, vii, ix, 9, 12, 35, 107, 151, 153, 154, 158
sister, 48, 49, 50, 51, 53, 55, 60, 65, 101, 106, 110, 125, 144, 155, 175, 177, 181
sisters, vi, vii, 3, 6, 35, 42, 46, 64, 72, 78, 79, 125, 133, 138, 139, 164, 182, 183
situation, 79, 80, 117, 118, 123, 130
Skydiving, 145

song, x, 9, 10, 12, 14, 15, 19, 107, 117, 154, 159, 171, 173, 174, 177, 188
songwriter, 9, 12, 14, 35, 107, 196
soul, iii, x, 14, 20, 21, 39, 79, 107, 111, 117, 119, 122, 123, 128, 158, 166, 178, 180, 192
special, xi, 10, 11, 13, 14, 36, 37, 38, 39, 46, 65, 71, 96, 99, 123, 126, 137, 139, 163, 168, 178
St. Matthews, 77, 102
state, 22, 59, 60, 72, 77, 81, 84, 86, 87, 94, 109, 117, 119, 121, 162, 163, 168, 172, 176
Steve Martin, 50
stories, v, x, 1, 2, 20, 28, 55, 56, 65, 81, 158, 187
story, iv, 1, 2, 9, 10, 12, 29, 42, 43, 51, 71, 82, 84, 88, 89, 94, 97, 101, 104, 105, 107, 108, 110, 112, 113, 115, 133, 138, 140, 156, 157, 172, 181, 184, 188, 190, 191, 196
stranger, 15, 20, 34, 110, 111

stressed, 116, 117
strive each day, 19
struggle, 52, 153, 154, 169
struggles, 9, 25, 52, 56, 135, 143, 158, 180
struggling, viii, 41, 50, 137, 142, 170
successful, 26, 135, 141
surroundings, 29, 31
symbolism, 36, 39
talents, ix, 11, 23, 43
tears, vi, xiii, 2, 10, 12, 47, 48, 49, 50, 53, 54, 55, 63, 74, 75, 80, 107, 108, 110, 111, 113, 115, 121, 122, 126, 128, 137, 138, 152, 183
Thank you, ii, iii, iv, v, vi, vii, viii, ix, x, 96, 199
thankful, 5, 37, 43, 56, 72, 122, 133, 162, 176, 180, 183, 189
thanksgiving, 3, 19, 83
The Power, 166
thoughts on life, 1
Tim McGraw, vii, 14, 188
time, iv, v, vi, vii, x, xi, 2, 3, 5, 6, 9, 10, 12, 13, 14, 17, 18, 21, 22, 29, 34, 35, 36, 38, 41, 42, 43, 45, 46, 47, 48, 49, 51, 52, 54, 55, 56, 59, 60, 61, 62, 63, 64, 68, 69, 72, 73, 74, 77, 79, 81, 82, 83, 84, 87, 90, 92, 93, 94, 102, 109, 116, 117, 118, 119, 120, 123, 125, 126, 128, 130, 131, 132, 135, 136, 137, 138, 140, 141, 142, 143, 144, 150, 151, 154, 155, 156, 157, 161, 162, 165, 167, 168, 172, 181, 182, 183, 189, 191, 196, 198
timeless, 29, 139, 183
together, iv, vi, vii, ix, xii, 1, 2, 5, 19, 25, 27, 36, 38, 41, 45, 46, 47, 48, 53, 60, 61, 62, 63, 65, 69, 71, 72, 74, 77, 78, 82, 91, 93, 94, 105, 107, 111, 112, 113, 115, 116, 125, 126, 133, 135, 137, 138, 143, 150, 159, 164, 165, 172, 175, 181, 182, 183, 190
Tony Robbins, 29, 30, 118, 168, 171
Toronto, 190, 191
traditions, iv, 11, 35, 65, 133, 190
transformation, 31
traumatic, 76

trials and tribulations, 20, 124, 181, 184, 198, 199
true passion, vii
Trusting, 31
Turner Station, 87, 88, 103
UK Basketball, 135
uncontrollable, 50
understanding, 2, 11, 28, 74
unhappy, 74, 116
unhealthy, 82, 116
universe, 22, 23, 80, 85, 87, 118, 119, 153, 159, 160, 161, 166, 175, 177, 180
values, iv
Vietnamese, 100, 101
vision, 60, 63, 133, 141, 169
Vision Boards, 170
visualize, 23, 27, 141, 170
vivid, 23, 27, 40, 60, 62
Vivotrol, 170
walk in my footsteps, 187
Walk in my footsteps, 194, 195
Walk in my Footsteps, x
walks among us every day, x
water, 23, 37, 46, 47, 50, 92, 118, 119, 127, 128, 161, 170, 171, 173, 178, 179
Waterway Park, 171, 177
wife, v, 18, 37, 55, 67, 68, 71, 72, 73, 76, 78, 80, 81, 83, 84, 87, 88, 90, 95, 97, 99, 102, 104, 105, 106, 107, 108, 110, 113, 117, 120, 126, 127, 128, 129, 182
Wildcats, v, 135, 137, 140, 141, 147, 150
win, 13, 79, 123, 141, 160
wisdom, iv, 124
wish, 4, 5, 6, 13, 26, 37, 52, 69, 75, 133, 163, 178, 189, 198
work, v, viii, 22, 51, 52, 54, 61, 67, 69, 71, 73, 75, 76, 77, 78, 79, 81, 84, 85, 86, 88, 90, 91, 92, 93, 102, 109, 112, 113, 115, 116, 119, 122, 126, 128, 129, 135, 136, 142, 151, 152, 153, 154, 156, 157, 158, 162, 166, 173, 191, 196
world, vi, vii, x, xii, 1, 5, 9, 10, 18, 19, 23, 26, 27, 31, 37, 38, 39, 41, 45, 48, 51, 52, 54, 69, 79,

     82, 88, 89, 104, 119,
     120, 124, 153, 159,
     161, 163, 164, 166,
     168, 177, 187, 194
wrap around porch, 40,
     83, 87, 101, 104, 120,
     132
Your dreams, 28

yourself, 20, 21, 22, 23,
     26, 28, 31, 36, 39, 43,
     78, 79, 81, 87, 117,
     127, 129, 130, 131,
     141, 142, 152, 158,
     160, 161, 163, 166,
     168, 169, 170, 174,
     199

Manufactured by Amazon.ca
Bolton, ON